Homemade Soap For Complete Beginners

Jemima .B Santiago

All rights reserved. Copyright © 2023 Jemima .B Santiago

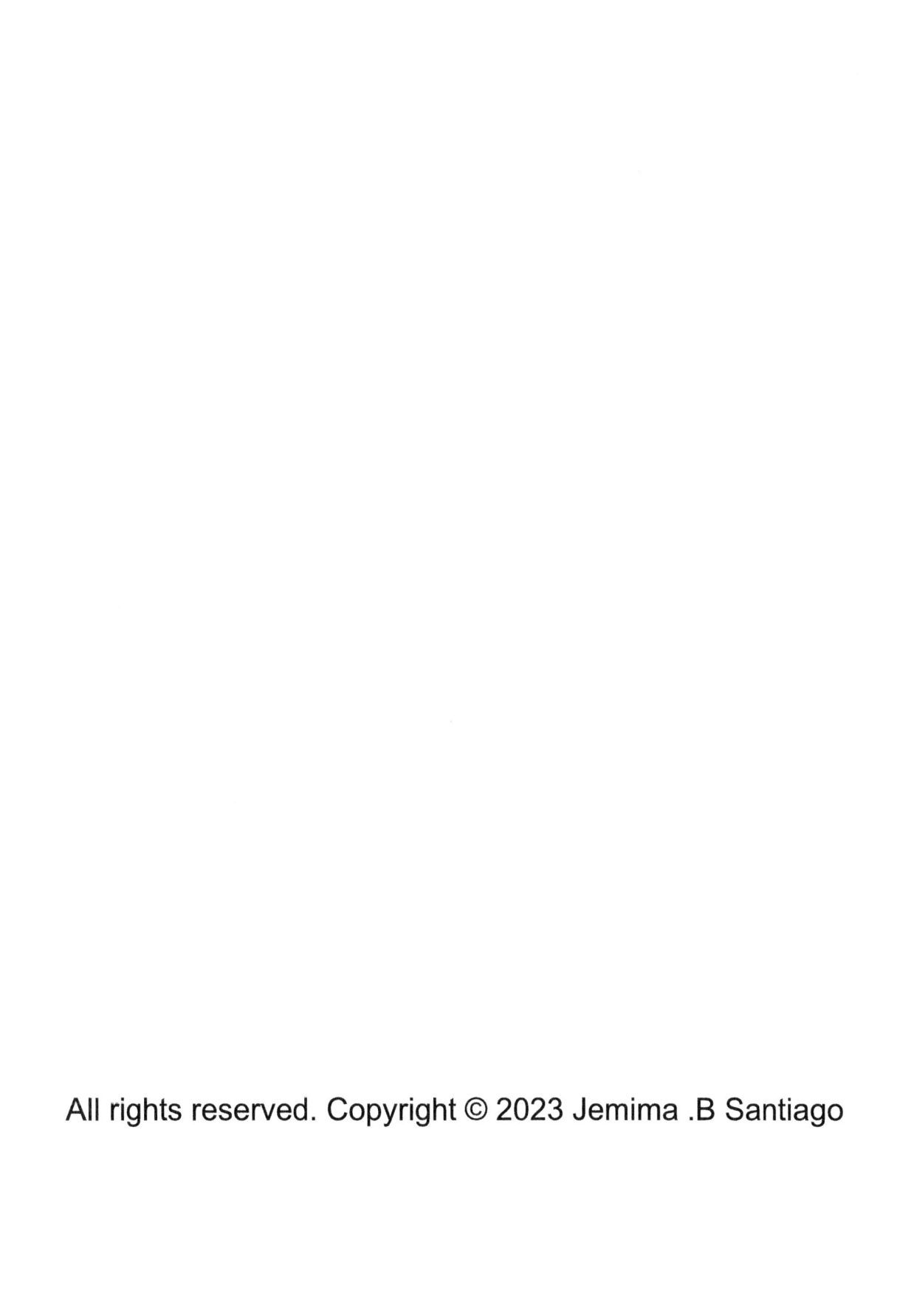

COPYRIGHT © 2023 Jemima .B Santiago

All rights reserved.

No part of this book must be reproduced, stored in a retrieval system, or shared by any means, electronic, mechanical, photocopying, recording, or otherwise, without written permission from the publisher.

Every precaution has been taken in the preparation of this book; still the publisher and author assume no responsibility for errors or omissions. Nor do they assume any liability for damages resulting from the use of the information contained herein.

Legal Notice:

This book is copyright protected and is only meant for your individual use. You are not allowed to amend, distribute, sell, use, quote or paraphrase any of its part without the written consent of the author or publisher.

Introduction

This is an informative guide that delves into the fascinating world of soap making from scratch. The book starts with a historical overview of soapmaking, providing readers with a context for this age-old craft. It emphasizes the importance of safety procedures and outlines the essential soap making equipment needed to embark on this creative journey.

The book explores various methods of making soap, offering detailed instructions for each process. From cold process soap making to melt-and-pour techniques, readers are given the knowledge to choose the method that best suits their preferences and skill level. Additionally, the guide covers how to incorporate scents, colors, and other ingredients to create personalized soap recipes.

The section on recipes offers a range of soap-making options, providing readers with tried-and-true formulas to get started. It also encourages readers to explore their creativity by explaining how to adjust batch sizes and create their own unique soap recipes. Addressing allergy considerations and frequently asked questions, the book ensures that readers are well-prepared and informed throughout their soap-making journey.

For those interested in liquid soap, the book provides a separate section dedicated to the art of making homemade liquid soap. It includes a historical background on liquid soap, safety precautions, detailed instructions, and a variety of liquid soap recipes to experiment with.

Moving beyond soap, the book extends its expertise to homemade body butter and lotion for beginners. It offers an exploration of the history of lotions and body butters, different types of lotions, safety measures, and ingredient understanding. With recipes, batch size adjustments, and the ability to create personalized formulations, this section empowers readers to craft their own skincare products.

Finally, the book addresses frequently asked questions and allergy considerations for both soap making and lotion creation, ensuring a well-rounded understanding of the topics. Overall, this book is a valuable resource for those looking to dive into the world of soap and skincare product creation, offering guidance and inspiration for crafting homemade creations.

Contents

Book 1: "Homemade Soap ForBeginners" 1
    CHAPTER 1: HISTORY OFSOAPMAKING 2
    CHAPTER 2: SAFETYPROCEDURES 5
    CHAPTER 3: SOAP MAKINGEQUIPMENT 7
    CHAPTER 4: DIFFERENT METHODS OF MAKING SOAP 9
    CHAPTER 5: INSTRUCTIONS FOREACH PROCESS 14
    CHAPTER 6: ADDING SCENT, COLOR & OTHER INGREDIENTS 27
    CHAPTER 7: RECIPES 31
    CHAPTER 8: CREATING YOUROWN RECIPES 42
    CHAPTER 9: HOW TO ADJUSTBATCH SIZES 44
    CHAPTER 10: ALLERGYCONSIDERATIONS 45
    CHAPTER 11: SOAP MAKINGFAQ'S 46

Book 2: "Homemade Liquid SoapFor Beginners" 51
    CHAPTER 1: HISTORY OFLIQUID SOAP 52
    CHAPTER 2: LIQUID SOAPMAKING SAFETY 57
    CHAPTER 3: INSTRUCTIONS FORLIQUID SOAP 59
    CHAPTER 4: HOW TO ADDOTHER INGREDIENTS 63
    CHAPTER 5: LIQUID SOAPRECIPES 67
    CHAPTER 6: HOW TO CREATERECIPES 84
    CHAPTER 7: HOW TO PACKAGEAND LABEL LIQUID SOAP 86
    CHAPTER 8: LIQUIDSOAPMAKING FAQ'S 88
    CHAPTER 9: ALLERGYCONSIDERATIONS 91

Book 3: "Homemade Body Butter& Lotion For Beginners" 93
    CHAPTER 1: HISTORY OFLOTION & BODY BUTTER 94

CHAPTER 2: DIFFERENT TYPES OF LOTIONS 96
CHAPTER 3: SAFETY & SANITATION PROCEDURES 100
CHAPTER 4: UNDERSTANDING THE INGREDIENTS 103
CHAPTER 5: ADDITIVES 106
CHAPTER 6: HOW TO MAKE LOTION, BODY BUTTER & CREAMS 133
CHAPTER 7: RECIPES 137
CHAPTER 8: HOW TO ADJUST BATCH SIZES 147
CHAPTER 9: CREATING YOUR OWN RECIPES 148
CHAPTER 10: FAQ'S 150

Book 1: "Homemade Soap For Beginners"

CHAPTER 1: HISTORY OF SOAPMAKING

Like many things soap was discovered by accident and there is not very much documentation about its' early production and use. Most of the information is anecdotal and passed down through oral tradition. The story goes that the dripping fat from a cooked animal mixed with ashes of the fire used to cook it. Probably due to rain, this mixture made its' way down the hill into the Tiber River, where people from the village did their laundry. The women noticed that when the mixture was present the clothes were easier to wash and were cleaner. The village was Sapo and that is thought to be the origin of the name of the product, soap.

The basic method for making soap at this time was to combine fat and potash from the fire. The first recipe for soap was found on Sumerian clay tablets dating to 2500BC. The recipe used potash, fat and water. The potash and water would be boiled and fat was stirred in and mixed until it dissolved. There is not any more information about how to finish the mixture or how to use it. We can only guess that people recognized that cleaning properties of soap and continued to use it to clean clothes.

Soap making first appeared in Pompeii, where a soap factory with soap bars was discovered in the ruins. While the Romans are credited with discovering soap, they did not use it for bathing. These early forms of soap were too harsh for the skin. The soap was used for laundry. Soap is still considered a detergent today.

Even through the Middle Ages, when bathing was considered unsanitary, soap was still used for washing clothes. Recipes were not written down, but rather passed down through word of mouth. During the 18th century bathing became popular as people began to develop better lifestyles and accumulate wealth. Due to increased demand, advances in soap making began happening at a very rapid pace. People wanted soaps to use in their baths and soap makers created new types of soaps to meet the needs of their customers. Different regions began using different ingredients in their soaps, based on what they had available to use. Vegetable oils were used in southern Europe, while cow fat was used in northern Europe. In the New World, early Americans perfected the method to make lye. They let water drip through the ashes and collected the lye as it leached off in a separate container. They used eggs to measure the potency of the solution, if the egg floated it was too strong, if it sunk all the way to the bottom it was too weak, it need to sink halfway.

Soap is made by combining fat and lye. As the most readily available source of fat came from animals, soap was typically made when animals were butchered. Most people would make a year worth of soap during the slaughter. Regional soaps were made using the fats from different animals.

In America commercial soap making began in the 19th century.

During the 18th century the demand for soap came at a time when there was a shortage of potash due to over cutting in the forests and a lack of trees. Soap makers began experimenting with new methods to make soap. In 1790, Frenchman Nicholas Leblanc discovered a process of converting common salt to an alkali. Leblancs' soap making method was to use salt, sulfuric acid, limestone, and coal to produce soda. Then the sodium carbonate was extracted and crystallized. By the 19th century this was the most popular method of making soap. This process while being easier had many disadvantages as it produced dangerous chemicals and was creating pollution.

In 1811, Augustin Jean Fresenel, discovered the ammonia-soda process. He combined common salt with ammonia and carbon dioxide to create bicarbonate soda. The soda was then heated and combined with fat. This process quickly became the main method for producing soap and is still used today. Other chemical advances at this time also contributed to the improvement of the soap making process and to how the soap turned out. As soap became a business; recipes and routines were established. The days of trial and error were over.

Whether produced commercially or at home soap making is considered a dangerous and smelly process. While you must take some precautions, it is a safe craft to practice. Soap manufacturers today still use the methods pioneered during the 18th and 19th centuries to make soap. Most commercial soap is made using animals fats, unless otherwise indicated on the label.

By adding colorants, dyes, perfumes and additional oils soaps today are radically different than the soaps of just 100 years ago. Even though soap is made using lye and harsh chemicals, the amounts and type of fat that are used make soap safe and gentle enough for a baby's skin.

Crafting soap at home has a rich tradition and there are many people who have started making soap at home for themselves or as a hobby. Many have also turned it into a successful small home based business. Making soap at home requires that you have a workspace, it doesn't have to be a dedicated workspace, but does have to be clutter free and organized on soap making day. You do need some equipment but you can use regular kitchen items such as a glass jar for mixing your lye and water solution, and a heavy bottomed pot or large glass bowl to melt your oils in. You can also use items from the recycling bin for soap molds. While there are many soap making suppliers who sell specialty equipment and ingredients you can find most ingredients at your local grocery. Making soap does not have to be complicated or use hard to find ingredients.

If you can follow a simple recipe, you can make soap. Learning how to correctly measure and combine the ingredients will ensure that your soap is safe for use. Soap making combines science, with art and creativity. You do need to follow some basic safety precautions to protect your skin, eyes and counters. With proper care soap making is a relaxing, rewarding and fun craft.

CHAPTER 2: SAFETY PROCEDURES

Soap making is a fun and rewarding craft to practice. Many of the methods used to make soap at home involve a instigating a chemical reaction or applying heat. By knowing the safety precautions you should take for the method of soap making you are using you will ensure that you can continue to make soap for years to come.

Read the recipe or instructions all the way through before you begin. Gather all of the equipment and ingredients you will need. Often you can replace ingredients or use common household or kitchen items when making soap. But this is much easier done, before you start making soap, than when you are halfway through.

Be Organized: Know the ingredients and tools that you will need before you start. Lay everything out and have things within easy reach. Having to stop mid way through a task to get an ingredient or a tool is time consuming and can be frustrating.

Have a clean area free of clutter. Even a small workspace can be more efficient if things are tidy and put away. When you are making soap, make sure you just have your soap making equipment and ingredients.

Spills are bound to happen so make sure you protect work surfaces and the floor. Lay down old towels, sheets or newspapers to protect the work surface and the floor.

Make sure your equipment is clean and in good working order. You will want your mixing containers, measuring tools and molds to be clean and dry.

Measure out your ingredients. Having your ingredients pre-measured will make the soap making process much easier, especially if something happens that you were not expecting.

Label any containers that you will have the lye in so no one mistakes it for a drinking beverage. Keep lye out of the reach of children and pets. Lye is a chemical and can be harmful and dangerous, but if used properly and with caution it is safe. Review the procedure for mixing the lye before you mix it and make sure you wear the proper safety protection: safety glasses and gloves. You can protect your clothing by wearing an apron. Be sure to keep a bottle of white vinegar, this will neutralize lye if needed.

Once you begin making soap, do not leave the oils on the stove unattended with the heat on. Make sure your oils are out of the reach of children and pets.

If possible work when your house is quiet, so you can focus and concentrate. This is especially true if this is your first time making soap, as you will be doing new things. Allow some extra time as well, so you don't feel hurried or rushed. By keeping a clean workspace, stocked with all of the equipment that you need and pre-measured ingredients, you will ensure that you are a successful soap maker.

CHAPTER 3: SOAP MAKING EQUIPMENT

You don't really need fancy or special equipment to make soap. You can probably find most of the things you need right in your kitchen. You can use heat resistant plastic, although stainless steel is preferred. You can use glass, but be mindful that you will be using oils and if you drop a glass container it can break, resulting in the loss of the oil and the container. The chemical reaction of the lye can reach temperatures of up to 200 degrees and can stay there for an extended period of time, so it is important that the container can handle that amount of heat, as well as the caustic alkaline mixture. When you do invest and buy soap making equipment, buy quality tools that you can use for a long time.

YOU'LL NEED THESE BASICS TO GET STARTED:

-Good Scale: Accurate measurement of ingredients is crucial to making sure that your soap turns out properly and that you can make your soap the same quality every time. Look for a scale that measures fractions of an ounce so you can weigh essential oils and herbs for small batches.

-Safety Gear: Proper safety gear is a must. Buy quality safety eyewear and gloves. Having glasses that fit properly and are comfortable ensures that you will wear them, the same goes for gloves, if your gloves are loose fitting they will get in the way and you will be less inclined to wear them. Always wear safety glasses and gloves to protect your eyes and skin.

-Large heat-resistant plastic or glass container: This will be used to mix the lye in. Always clearly label this container and keep it out of the reach of children and pets.

-Large long handled mixing spoon: This can be made of stainless steel or plastic. You'll need this to stir the lye solution.

-Soap Pot: Depending on the batch sizes you'll be making, find an appropriate sized pot. You will use your soap pot to melt your oils and to blend the soap. A large 8 to 12 quart stainless steel pot should accommodate large batches of soap.

-Thermometer: using an easy to read and easy to calibrate thermometer will let you monitor the temperatures of the lye mixture and of the oils you are using.

-Measuring Spoons: you will need these to measure essential oils, additives, dyes or colorants.

-Stick Blender: These are essential to quickly and thoroughly blend the oils with the lye solution. A stick blender also ensures that any additives will get thoroughly blended in and not clump together.

-Ladle: A ladle will make transferring your soap mixture from the pot to the molds much easier.

-Small mixing spoons and mixing bowls: These will be used to blend dyes or colorants into your soap mixture.

-Soap Molds: You can use many different containers as a soap mold. Boxes or round containers make great molds as you can slice the soap into bars or rounds. Make sure the molds are able to handle the heat and do not leak. You can line molds with plastic wrap or freezer paper.

-Rubber Spatula: This will be used to scrape down the sides of the soap pot, so you can use all of the soap mixture. It can also be used to smooth the top of the soap once it is in the mold.

-Cleaning Towels: There are bound to be a few spills, so having some cleaning towels handy will make clean up easier.

-Note: The items you need from this list will depend on which soap making process you choose. The different soap making methods are covered in the following chapters.

When you make your first batch, read the recipe and make sure that you have the right equipment. You need everything to be the right size, to accommodate the oils and lye solution. Some recipes may have oils added at different times so you may need an extra container or two. As you make soap you will learn which tools and equipment you like and you can customize your set up to your needs.

CHAPTER 4: DIFFERENT METHODS OF MAKING SOAP

There are many different methods of making soap. Each one offers it challenges and benefits depending on your available time, your budget and your skill. All of the methods allow you to be as creative as you want to be. You can always make colorful, bubbly wonderful smelling soap however you choose to do it. As you try each method and make more soap, you will find the method that works for you and the type of soap you most like to make and use.

This chapter will give you an overview of the different methods of soap making so that you can choose the methods that best fits your needs. The next chapter will provide instructions for each soap making method.

MELT AND POUR SOAP MAKING METHOD:

Perhaps the simplest soap making method, melt and pour is a very straightforward process. You purchase a pre-made soap base that you melt (according to the manufacturers directions). Then you can add colorants, scented oils, and additives such as herbs, oatmeal, loofah or other items. Then you pour the base into your chosen molds and let it cool and harden. Melt and pour soap can be used once it is hardened, so it is a good choice if you want to use your soap right away or give it to friends or family as a quick gift.

Melt and pour soaps offer you a wonderful opportunity to be very creative with color and design. The only limits are your creativity.

COLD PROCESS METHOD

Cold process soap making is more involved than melt and pour. This method gives you the flexibility to choose the ingredients in your soap. You will transform basic ingredients using a recipe into soap. Cold process soap making combines science and creativity. The chemical process of saponification transforms your oils and lye into soap. Once you mix the lye with water it will get very hot, the heat will remain due to the chemical reaction. You can add other ingredients such as dyes or colorants, herbs, oats, honey and scents. The chemical reaction can affect some of the ingredients that you use, such as fats and oils.

For active soap-makers, cold process soap is the most popular method. Soap makers get the most control over the ingredients and once you have your systems and recipes in place the process gets much easier and faster.

HOT PROCESS METHOD

Hot process method soap making is very similar to cold process. By heating the oils and other ingredients used in the soap you can speed up saponification process. You can use heat sources such as the oven, microwave or cooktop. Hot process is the most famous traditional method. It is how people have made soap for centuries. Hot process soap cures quickly, but can be tricky to remove from the mold.

MILLED SOAP METHOD

Milling soap gives it a denser finer texture, resulting in a longer lasting soap. Milled soap has become popular because it often contains extra ingredients that make the skin feel clean and moisturized. Milled soap is made by cutting up or shredding soap that you have already made; and then melting them. You also soak the cut up soap in milk or water until it dissolves. Once you melt your base, you add extra oils, fats, scents or colors. This method is very similar to melt and pour, except you have made the soap base. You can use this method to salvage a batch of soap that didn't quite work out.

CHAPTER 5: INSTRUCTIONS FOR EACH PROCESS

MELT AND POUR SOAP INSTRUCTIONS

Melt and pour is the easiest of all the soap making methods. It is also the safest and is fun for the novice and expert soap maker alike. Melt and pour is a great way to introduce kids to the art of soap making without having to worry about exposure to lye. Even the least crafty person can make beautiful soap without stress. Experienced soap makers can focus on being creative with color and aromas while making patterns and embedding decorative items in the soap.

STEPS TO COMPLETE MELT AND POUR SOAP:

-Lay out all of the tools and equipment that you will be using to make your soap. Make sure that all of your equipment is clean and dry.

-Determine the mold or molds that you want to use. Fill them with water and pour the water into a measuring cup, this will let you know how much of the melt and pour base you need to melt.

-Measure out the amount of soap base you need, and cut it into small pieces so it will melt easily and evenly.

-You can melt the soap base on the stovetop in a double boiler or in the microwave. Depending on how much soap you are melting it will take more or less time to melt completely. If you melt it in the microwave, check on it every 30 seconds, you don't want it to get so hot that it boils over. If you melt it on the stovetop use a double boiler and stir it frequently to prevent it from scorching. The soap does not need to boil, it just needs to be melted into a liquid. If there are a few small pieces floating and the mixture is getting too hot, you can stir until they are melted.

-Once the base is melted you can add in any dyes, colorants, oils or butters, scents or essential oils. Add your ingredients and stir thoroughly to combine.

-Once you have added your additives, you can pour your soap into the molds. Allow the soap to cool. Have your molds in a place were they can set up undisturbed. The soap does not need to cure, but it does need to harden completely before being removed from the mold. If the soap is completely hardened it will be easier to remove from the mold.

Melt and pour offers excellent opportunities for creating very colorful and creative patterns in the soap. You can make a soap loaf and cut bars that reveal vibrant and exciting patterns.

SUSPENDED SOAPS

Suspended soaps use a combination of colored, opaque and clear soap. By mixing up the different types of soap you can create really fun soaps. The soaps you make can be as simple or complex as you can imagine.

By combing colored clear, clear, opaque and colored opaque, you can create countless combinations and patterns. Choose one type to be your base and use the other two in chunks, grated, slivers or molded pieces. You can also layer two types of soap and use suspended pieces of all 3. Refrigerating the pieces you submerge will help them keep a distinct pattern when submerged in the hot soap base.

LAYERED AND MARBLED MELT AND POUR SOAP

You can make wonderfully beautiful layered and marbled soaps by pouring clear melt and pour soap and opaque melt and pour soap bases into a mold either in layers: letting the first layer cool and set before adding the next layer, or by pouring them at the same time and gently swirling them together. You can choose to pour these soaps in whatever color combination you like. Note, you need to pour soap bases of the same type so they stick together.

SUSPENDED ITEMS

You can suspend items in your soap, so they appear to be floating. You will do this after you have placed the soap into the mold and it has begun to cool and thicken. Take your item and press it into the soap where you want it to be. If you do it before the soap has cooled enough the item will sink to the bottom of the mold, remove the item and try gain in a few minutes. If the soap has thickened too much you can simply re-melt the soap and start again. Once you have your items suspended allow the soap to harden completely before removing the soap from the mold.

COLD PROCESS SOAP INSTRUCTIONS

Knowing exactly what is going into your most frequently used skin care product is definitely the major appeal of making soap. Cold process and hot process differ from melt and pour, because you control all of the ingredients that are used. You can create a moisturizing, cleansing, fragrant, all natural soap with quality ingredients. Quality handmade soaps make amazing gifts as well.

Cold process soap has a short prep time and a long cure time. The long wait can be frustrating if you're in a hurry to use your soap; however, the long cure is necessary to produce the best quality soap. You will spend 1-2 hours making a batch of cold process soap and then an additional 4-6 weeks to cure the soap. During the cure process the soap evaporates all of the water and the soap completes the saponification process. Allowing the soap to dry and cure creates a long lasting hard bar of soap. It is important to allow the soap to saponify so the chemical reaction of the lye water and fat can be completed. You can use cold process soap within a week of it being made, just don't be surprised if it melts and falls apart easily.

STEPS TO COMPLETE COLD PROCESS SOAP:

-Choose your recipe and gather all of the ingredients, tools and equipment you need.

-Prepare your mold or molds according to the directions in your recipe.

-Wearing your safety gear, mix your lye and water. Always add the lye to the water, pouring water on top of lye can activate the lye and the mixture can splatter on you. The mixture will heat up very quickly and create fumes, do not stand with your face directly over the container. Mix the solution in ventilated area and do not breathe in the fumes. Stir the solution very well until the lye dissolves. You will need to monitor the temperature of the lye solution, so make sure you have a calibrated and easy to read thermometer. The solution will be ready to use when the temperature is between 100-120 degrees.

-Measure your oils, and melt them. You can melt the oils on the stovetop in a double boiler, on very low heat or in the microwave. Just make sure that you check on the oils so they don't scorch or boil over. The oils need to be in the same temperature range as the lye, between 100-120 degrees.

-Prepare any colorants, scents or additives.

-Once the lye solution is at the right temperature, wearing your safety gear, slowly pour the lye mixture into the melted oils stirring constantly. If you use a stick blender (recommended) keep the base of the blender submerged in the soap pot. Until saponification occurs the mixture is still caustic and you do not want the blender to splatter the oil and lye mixture around. The mixture will be become cloudy and then begin to thicken. Continue stirring until the mixture reaches trace (trace is when the mixture becomes thick like pudding). You can tell the mixture has reached trace if your remove the blender from the mixture (not running) and it leaves an imprint in the soap.

-Once the soap has reached trace you can add your additives. Add each additive and mix thoroughly until everything is completely incorporated. You will need to work quickly, as once the soap reaches trace it will thicken up quickly.

-Once you've incorporated all of your ingredients, you can pour the soap into the mold/molds. Allow the soap to set up in the mold until it is hardened. Remove the soap from the mold cut it into bars and allow it to cure in a well ventilated area for up to 6 weeks before using.

HOT PROCESS SOAP INSTRUCTIONS

Hot process soap has the same instructions as cold process soap up until the point of trace. In cold process, at trace you will add all of your additives and pour the soap into the mold. With hot process at trace you will cook the soap, turning it from a raw and caustic mixture into saponified soap. Hot process soap still needs to cure, but not nearly as long as cold process. Many people prefer cold process, as cooking the soap and seeing it transform into a gelled state and having to test it for doneness is a little intimidating. Both methods make excellent soap with interesting and unique variation. Hot process bars tend to be more rustic while cold process bars seem to be smoother and more refined. When you make hot process soap you can use your soap more quickly than you can when you make cold process. You will have about 2-3 hours of soap making time and up to 2 weeks of curing time. You can use any cold process soap making recipe to make hot process soap.

STEPS TO COMPLETE HOT PROCESS SOAP:

-Chose your recipe, gather all of the ingredients, tools and equipment.
-Prepare any colorants, scents or additives that you will be using.
-Prepare your mold or molds according to the directions in your recipe.
-Wearing your safety gear, mix your lye and water. Always add the lye to the water, pouring water on top of lye can activate the lye and the mixture can splatter and splash. The mixture will heat up very quickly and create fumes, do not stand with your face directly over the container. Mix the solution in ventilated area and do not breathe in the fumes. Stir the solution very well until the lye dissolves. You will need to monitor the temperature of the lye solution, so make sure you have a calibrated and easy to read thermometer. The solution will be ready to use when the temperature is between 100-120 degrees.
-Weigh or measure your ingredients and melt your oils. You can use a soap pot on the stove top or you can use a slow cooker. Melt the oils. Just make sure that you check on the oils so they don't scorch or boil over. The oils need to be in the same temperature range as the lye, between 100-120 degrees. If you are going to use a colorant you can add it to the oils now. You can ladle some of the melted oil out of the pot mix it with the colorant and then combine it well with all the oil, you can use the stick blender for this.
-Once the lye solution is at the right temperature, wearing your safety gear, slowly pour the lye mixture into the melted oils stirring constantly. If you use a stick blender (recommended) keep the base of the blender submerged in the soap pot. Until saponification occurs the mixture is still caustic and you do not want the blender to splatter the oil and lye mixture around.
-The mixture will be become cloudy and then begin to thicken. Continue stirring until the mixture reaches trace. Trace is when the mixture becomes thick like pudding. You can tell you have reached trace if your remove the blender from the mixture (not running) and it leaves an imprint in the soap.
-Once the soap has reached trace you can apply the hot process, by maintaining a low consistent heat. Place a lid on the soap and set a timer

for 15 minutes (you can check on it every few minutes if you like, it helps to have a glass lid so you don't let the heat escape).

-The soap is going to change as it cooks, it may look as though it has separated, it may rise and bubble (always use a large pot to prevent the soap from overflowing out of the pot). You can gently stir the soap with a spoon to release air and it should settle back down in the pot. You will cook the soap until it gels. Then you will set the timer and cook it for another 15 minutes.

-In order to tell if the soap is done, use pH testing strips (you can normally find these in a pool supply store). Dip the testing strip into your mixture and let it sit. Check the color of the strip to get the pH reading (this can take several minutes). The goal is to get a pH between 8-10. If the pH is high let it cook for 15 minutes and test again. Complete this process until the pH of your mixture is between 8-10. You can now add any scents or additives and blend well to combine everything. Note the temperature of the soap when you add your fragrances, if the soap is above the flashpoint of the oils you will loose some of the aromas and notes of your scent and may have to add extra.

-When the soap is done you will want to work quickly adding scents and additives as the soap will begin to harden quite quickly.

-Pour the soap into the prepared mold. You will want to tap the mold a few times on the counter to remove any air bubbles. You can use a rubber spatula to smooth the top of the soap once it is in the mold.

-Allow the soap to set up in the mold until it is hardened. Remove the soap from the mold cut it into bars and allow it to cure in a well ventilated area for up to 2 weeks before using.

MILLED SOAP INSTRUCTIONS

Milled soap can be made from a basic unscented, uncolored batch of either cold process soap or hot process soap. You can re-batch scented colored soap if you want to, to enrich the scent or make it more moisturizing by adding additional oils or butters. You may also use a batch of hot process or cold process soap that didn't turn out as well as you thought it would. Or use the trimmed left over pieces from making bars. Using completely cured and finished soap to make milled soap will let you use the soap as soon as the bars harden.

STEPS TO COMPLETE MILLED SOAP:

-Chose your recipe, gather all of the ingredients, tools and equipment.
-Prepare any colorants, scents or additives that you will be using.
-Prepare your mold or molds according to the directions in your recipe.
-Grate or cut the soap into small uniform pieces. Melt the soap in a double boiler, microwave or a crockpot. Stir the melted soap very well, especially if you are using bits and pieces of other recipes. The soap does not need to be very hot, just melted uniformly.
-Once the soap is melted you can add colorants, oils, butters, essential oils, herbs, etc... Mix very well to combine these ingredients.
-Pour the soap into your prepared molds and allow it to harden. Once the soap hardens, remove from the mold and allow to cure. If you used cured soap to make your milled soap, the bars will be ready to use as soon as they harden, if you didn't use cured soap, you will have to let the soap cure for 1-2 weeks (hot processed soap) or 5-6 weeks (cold processed soap).

CHAPTER 6: ADDING SCENT, COLOR & OTHER INGREDIENTS

Typically scent, color and other ingredients go into the soap at the end of the process right before the soap is poured into the mold. As you are making a handmade crafted item, try to keep your ingredients simple and natural. There are many products available to soap-makers, you can use natural or synthetic scents and colorants. Natural products are typically safer to use and milder on the skin. Natural products can also add health benefits to your soap.

Scents

Essential oils make wonderful additions to soap, both for their medicinal and aromatic properties. Make sure you research all of the properties of essential oils as some of them can be skin irritants. Also due to their potency, make sure you measure them accurately and only use the amount called for in the recipe.

You may also use fragrance oils in your soap. Not all fragrance oils are synthetic, there are many all natural fragrance oils available. Read the ingredients and purchase your products from a reputable business.

COLOR

When you want to add color you can use many natural products such as cocoa powder, turmeric and other spices. These colorants are fun and typically color the soap in very light earth colors. You can purchase natural pigment colorants that will give your soap richer more vibrant color. Always measure you color accurately and combine it as directed by the recipe you are using. Adding color to your soap is fun and can let you be creative with marbling or mixing colors. Color can change through saponification and curing, keep detailed notes on the type and amount of color you used. This way you can track the effects and changes for future batches of soap you make.

OTHER INGREDIENTS

Milk makes soap very creamy. It can however be very tricky to use milk in soap. Due to the intense and sustained heat of the chemical reaction of the lye, the proteins and fats in the milk burn and the milk can turn a dark yellow or orange color. Because of this you may have problems getting your soap to trace and your soap can even smell burnt or like sour milk. There are still options if you want to add milk, you can freeze the milk until it is slushy and then slowly add the lye. You can also add milk after trace. You can use liquid milk or powdered milk. If you use powdered milk, dissolve it in a small amount of water or oil, to make it easier to incorporate into the soap.

Coffee, Tea and Juice can be used in your soap making imparting their color and aroma. Depending on the type of soap you want to make, you can use these liquids in the lye solution or add them in concentrated or powdered forms at trace.

Honey has amazing humectant and antimicrobial properties making it a wonderful ingredient for soap. Add honey at trace, mixing well to combine.

Exfoliants can be added to soap at trace. How much and which type of exfoliant depends on the purpose of the soap. An oatmeal face soap will have a small amount of very finely ground oatmeal, where a hand soap for gardeners may include quite a lot of cornmeal. You can add many different types of exfoliants to your soap: Ground spices, dried herbs and flowers, ground nuts, seeds or flowers. Add exfoliants at trace so they stay evenly suspended throughout the soap.

Botanicals make lovely additions to soap and lend texture, visual appeal and aroma. Add them at trace. Some common botanicals you can use include: lavender, chamomile, rose petals, citrus peel, parsley, green tea & mint.

Vitamins and Skin Nutrients help the skin to stay healthy and fight the effects of aging. Vitamins and Skin Nutrients that you can add at trace include: Vitamins A, C & E, B-Vitamins or B-Complex, Selenium, and Biotin. You can buy these in liquid form or grind up tablets.

CHAPTER 7: RECIPES

These recipes can be made using either cold process or hot process soap. You will want to follow the instructions as outlined for each process in Chapter 5. If you want to make one of these soaps to use as a soap base for milled soap, simply leave out the fragrances, essential oils, colorants or other additives.

Olive Soap

This is a lovely bubbly soap made with ingredients that you can find at your local grocery.

-Lye Solution: 4 oz. Lye and 8.5 oz. Water

-12 oz. Canola Oil

-8 oz. Coconut Oil

-8 oz. Olive Oil

At Trace add:

-1.6 oz. Orange Essential Oil

Coconut Soap

This makes a really hard bar of soap with lots of thick creamy bubbles.

-Lye Solution: 7.4 oz. Lye and 16 oz. Water

-16 oz. Coconut Oil

-16 oz. Palm Oil

-16 oz. Olive Oil

-2 oz. Castor Oil

At Trace add:

-2 oz. Lavender Essential Oil

- Sprinkle fresh shredded coconut (unsweetened) on top of soap mixture if desired

Cinnamon Honey Oat Soap

A wonderfully aromatic soap with big bubbles and mild exfoliating properties.

-Lye Solution: 7oz Lye and 18 oz. Water

-26 oz. Olive Oil

-10 oz. Coconut Oil

-6 oz. Almond Oil

-5 oz. Avocado Oil

-4 oz. Castor Oil

At Trace add:

-2 oz. Honey

-2 oz. Oats, ground

-1 Tablespoon Cinnamon

Castile Soap

A classic olive oil castile soap with the refreshing invigorating qualities of peppermint.

-Lye Solution: 7.3 oz. Lye and 17 oz. Water

-56 oz. Olive Oil

At Trace add:

-2.5 oz. Peppermint Essential Oil

Pineapple Coconut Soap

Due to the coconut milk this soap is extra creamy with thick lather and great big bubbles, the pineapple fragrance is sweet and summery.

-Lye Solution: 6.25 oz. Lye and 14 oz. Coconut Milk*

-16 oz. Coconut Oil

-14 oz. Olive Oil

-8 oz. Sunflower Oil

-6 oz. Safflower Oil

At Trace add:

-2 oz. Pineapple Fragrance

Calendula Soap

This mild soap is gentle enough for the most sensitive of skin, made with double strength Calendula tea, it makes a creamy lather and medium bubbles.

-Lye Solution: 5.75 oz. Lye and 13 oz of Double Strength Calendula Tea (cooled)

-21 oz. Olive Oil

-14 oz. Coconut Oil

-5 oz. Sunflower Oil

-2 oz. Castor Oil

Citrus Soap

Lightly colored with turmeric this refreshing citrusy soap leaves skin feeling refreshed and clean with lovely lather and bubbles.

-Lye Solution: 8.75 oz. Lye and 20 oz Double Strength Lemon Balm Tea (cooled)

-28 oz Olive Oil

-22 oz. Coconut Oil

-8 oz Sunflower Oil

-4 oz Castor Oil

At Trace add:

-2 teaspoons Lemon Essential Oil

-1 teaspoon Lime Essential Oil

-1 teaspoon Orange Essential oil

-1 Tablespoon Turmeric Powder

Carrot Mango Soap

Full of skin nutrients this is a wonderful facial soap, or for all over body use to nourish and replenish skin.

-Lye Solution: 12 oz. Lye, 10 oz. Carrot Juice and 16oz Water

-36 oz. Olive Oil

-24 oz. Coconut Oil

-22 oz. Palm Kernel Oil

-2 oz. Mango Butter

At Trace add:

-1 oz. Honey

-12 drops carrot Seed Essential Oil

-1 Tablespoon Mango Butter

-1 Tablespoon Rosehip Seed Oil

-1 Tablespoon Vitamin E

ALOE VERA SOAP

A very mild soap with excellent lather and cleansing abilities. You can add fragrance when you add the aloe vera gel at trace if you wish.

-Lye Solution: 6.5 oz. Lye and 9.5 oz. Water

-15 oz. Coconut Oil

-13 oz. Olive Oil

-10 oz. Palm Kernel Oil

-2.5 oz. Shea Butter

At Trace add:

-8 oz Aloe Vera Gel

TEA TREE OIL SOAP

A very refreshing soap with the amazing antiseptic and anti microbial properties of tea tree, this is an excellent hand soap.

-Lye Solution: 2.25 oz Lye and 6 oz. Water

-7 oz. Olive Oil

-5 oz. Coconut Oil

-2 oz. Sweet Almond Oil

-2 oz. Avocado Oil

At Trace add:

-36 oz Tea Tree Oil

CHAPTER 8: CREATING YOUR OWN RECIPES

After you've made a few recipes and have learned how to make soap you will want to continue to make progress and create your own recipes. You can create recipes based on the ingredients you can readily find in your area, or using ingredients that you order from a soap ingredient and equipment supplier. There are many online resources to help you when you make your own recipes. You will need to use a lye calculator to determine how much lye/water you need to saponify the fats/oils you use.

Creating your own recipes is very fun and the possibilities are endless. You can add colors, combine colors and submerge soap shapes to create visually beautiful soap. By mixing different fragrance or essential oils you can create soaps for use in aromatherapy or that just smell really good. All of the additives allow you a great amount of freedom to create unique and interesting soaps.

When you being to create your own recipes you will want to start out by choosing the base oils you want to use. The properties of your base oils will affect the quality, texture and lather of your finished bar of soap. You can mix and match oils to create creamy lather, lots of bubbles and moisturizing benefits. It all depends on what type of soap you want to make. How the oil affects the soap depends on its' fatty acid properties. When you make your own recipes you will learn to think about ingredients in terms of percentages. For instance you will use a set percentage of a certain oil, depending on how big the batch of soap you are making is, you can convert that percentage into an amount that you can measure and weigh.

You can use a lye calculator to determine how much lye and water (or other liquid) to use. You will need to know the types of oils and the weight. There are different types of lye available, so know if you are using powdered or liquid. The water or liquid is usually given as a range, and you can choose how much to use within the range given.

Many calculators will give you a % of excess fat and a percentage to superfat. If you have 0% of excess fat, you will need a superfat. During saponification the moisturizing properties of your oils and fats is cancelled out by the chemical reaction of the lye. By superfatting the soap you will ensure that your soap is creamy and moisturizing to the skin, not drying.

CHAPTER 9: HOW TO ADJUST BATCH SIZES

There are many ways to figure out what batch size your recipe needs to be. The easiest way to determine the size of your batch is to know how much soap your mold will hold. If you have purchased molds you will know the size and they should state the volume that they will hold. If you are improvising and using molds made from household items you can still easily figure out their volume. Line your mold and fill it with water, then pour the water into a measuring cup. If you are using more than one mold, add up all the amounts and that will tell you how much oil to use in your recipe.

When you create a recipe you want your oils to equal the volume of water it takes to fill your mold. By using a lye calculator you can add your oils and the calculator will tell you how much water and lye to use. Even though it seems like halving or doubling a batch would be fairly straightforward, always put your ingredients into a calculator to make sure you right proportions of lye and water for your recipe. By taking notes each time you make a batch of soap you will start to understand how all of the ingredients work together and which ingredients lend certain properties to your soap.

CHAPTER 10: ALLERGY CONSIDERATIONS

As 20% of Americans are affected by allergies, knowing the ingredients you use in your soap will help you to avoid triggering an allergic reaction in anyone that uses the soap you make. As homemade soap uses natural oils and ingredients it will be milder and more gentle on the skin.

Glycerin is a byproduct of homemade soap. Glycerin attracts moisture to the skin and keeps skin soft and moist. Commercial producers of soap extract the glycerin from their soap, making it harsh and drying.

Many commercially made soaps are actually detergents and are made with synthetic ingredients and fragrances that irritate skin and trigger allergic reactions. This is why keeping your ingredients simple and natural is a good idea. Even though the soap you make at home begins with a caustic solution, once it goes through saponification with the oils and cures, it is not.

CHAPTER 11: SOAP MAKING FAQ'S

CAN YOU MAKE SOAP WITHOUT LYE?

-No. You can't make soap at home without lye. Lye is perfectly safe to use at home with the proper safety precautions. Lye when combined with water, creates a chemical reaction that will bind with oils and fats in a process called saponification. When you follow the recipe using the correct amounts of all ingredients and follow the procedure and cure the soap, your homemade soap with be gentler and more mild than any commercially made soap you can buy at the store.

CAN I RECYCLE SOAP SCRAPS?

-Yes. You can recycle all of your soap scraps ones from your home made soap and even add in store bought. Grate the soap or cut it in small pieces, you can melt the soap in a slow cooker. Only add enough water to make a smooth liquid when all of the soap is melted. You can add any additives that you like including essential oils, fragrance, exfoliants, botanicals, extra fats and oils. Pour the soap into the mold and let it harden and cure until you have a dry new hard bar of soap.

I'M OVERWHELMED BY ALL THE TECHNICAL SCIENCE STUFF, CAN I MAKE SOAP?

-Yes. First thing you need to do is stop and take a deep breath. Making soap is very much like baking a cake. If you can bake a cake from a box mix, you can make melt and pour soap. If you can make a cake from scratch you can make cold process or hot process soap. Read the recipe and gather your ingredients and equipment before soap making day. Have your workspace cleaned and ready. If you can work undisturbed and can focus on soap making, you will be just fine.

HOW LONG WILL MY HOMEMADE SOAP LAST?

-Homemade soap will last a very long time when made correctly and stored properly. If you follow the recipe using correct proportions and store the soap in a clean dry area, it can be stored for years. For soap stored for an excessively long time or stored under extreme conditions (like extreme heat or cold) you may notice a decrease in the aroma or a fading of the color.

TIPS TO HELP IMPROVE YOUR SOAPS' LONGEVITY:

-Don't decrease the amount of lye.
-Don't add to much oil when super fatting.
-Don't put too many additives in your soap; ie fruits, plants, vegetables, herbs, or flour.
-Store your soap in a container that allows for ventilation.

IS HOMEMADE SOAP ALL NATURAL OR ORGANIC?

-Homemade soap can be made using as many all natural or organic ingredient as you are willing to find or can source. There are differences between all natural and organic products. Depending on where you get your ingredients from and their certification, your soap will either be all natural, organic or simply be a percentage of all natural or organic. When buying organic ingredients, make sure they have the proper documentation to back up that claim.

HOW IS HOMEMADE SOAP DIFFERENT FROM COMMERCIALLY PRODUCED SOAP?

-Handmade soap is much milder on the skin than commercially produced soap. Commercially produced soap removes the glycerin that is produced during the soap making process, unlike homemade soap which is full of glycerin that helps rejuvenate the skin.

WHAT IS THE DIFFERENCE BETWEEN COLORANTS, DYES AND PIGMENTS?

-The term colorants refers to both dyes and pigments. Either can be all natural or synthetic, just read the label.

CAN I USE NATURAL PRODUCTS TO COLOR MY SOAP?

-Yes many natural products can be used to color your soap such as; beet juice, turmeric, paprika, cocoa powder, tea and flowers. These ingredients can be added at trace.

WHEN CAN I ADD FRAGRANCE TO THE SOAP?

-Fragrance can be added once the soap is melted if you are making melt and pour soap, at trace if you are making cold process soap, after the gelling stage if you are making hot process soap, and once the soap is melted if you are making milled soap.

SHOULD I USE FRAGRANCE OILS OR ESSENTIAL OILS IN MY SOAP?

-You can use either or both. Many fragrance oils are all natural, although some contain synthetic fragrances. Fragrance oils are stabilized so the aroma may be stronger and last longer than essential oils. Essential oils often contain many healing properties that are good for the skin and the senses. Use the products that you like and that make your soap smell the way you want it to.

Disclaimer

While perfectly safe is used properly lye is a serious chemical. You need to make sure you follow safety protocols by wearing safety glasses, safety gloves, using the proper equipment, work in a well ventilated area and always add the lye to the water. By following these safety protocols you decrease any risks associated with using lye. Lye is very caustic until it has saponified with the oils used in soap making, should it come in contact with your skin it can easily be neutralized with white vinegar. Seek medical attention as it is appropriate for you if you need it. Always keep children and pets away from the work are and the lye solution. Always clearly label the lye solution. Keep the lye stored in a safe area.

When heating oils, use a heavy bottomed pot on the stove top, a large glass bowl in the microwave. Do not leave the oils unattended on the stovetop or in the microwave for extended periods of time. The oils only need to be warmed enough to melt. Keep children and pets away from work area and the heated oils.

While I have tested the recipes included in this book and have made them successfully, I cannot guarantee how they will turn out for you. I do not know the quality of the ingredients that you will be using, the type of equipment you have available or your skill level. Always measure and weigh your ingredients, take your time and work undisturbed if possible.

Soap making is a creative craft. I hope you enjoy making many wonderful bars of soap for years to come using all of the methods mentioned in this book.

This book about Soap Making is intended for entertainment purposes only. It is not intended to be and should not be taken as instruction. As with any craft, seek professional hands on instructional classes if you have any questions or concerns.

Book 2: "Homemade Liquid Soap For Beginners"

CHAPTER 1: HISTORY OF LIQUID SOAP

Liquid soap is one of the most convenient and versatile soaps available. It is easy to use and can be used for many different types of cleaning from personal to household and even industrial uses. Liquid soap is popular as it is easy to dispense and lathers almost immediately for hand washing. When used for laundry it dissolves easier than flake soap. When liquid soap became popular in the early 19th century it changed the way people cleaned. Prior to the invention of liquid soap people used bar soap or flaked bar soap for just about all cleaning situations.

In 1865 liquid soap was patented by soap maker William Shepphard. Liquid soap quickly became popular as it made cleaning easier. BJ Johnson started selling their liquid dish soap made from palm and olive oils, hence the name, Palmolive in 1898. The liquid dish soap was so popular the company changed their name to Palmolive. Over time other companies caught on to how many people appreciated liquid soap and products like Pin-sol and Tide were invented.

Commercially made liquid soaps were milder on the hands of people washing dishes and washing clothes on a washboard. Liquid soap lathered and bubbled easier and cleaned clothes and dishes without residue. Liquid soap was easier to use in hard water and cold water. So having a liquid soap really made a big difference in peoples lives.

As people began to understand the benefits of soap, soap making became a craft and there was even a soap manufacturing facility discovered amidst the ruins of Pompeii. Soap making skills and recipes were handed down from one soap maker to another for centuries. Practically every civilization on the planet was able to discover the cleaning effects of animal fat and ashes. Many early peoples used oils and fragrances to bathe with, these were later combined with soap ingredients to make soap similar to what we are familiar with today.

During the 18th century life began to become easier for many people and bathing became very fashionable. As the popularity of soap increased, the readily available ingredients decreased. Due to a construction explosion, trees were in high demand and potash was rare. During this time many processes were invented to make bar soap using other methods and ingredients. Scientists worked on formulas and applied chemistry and theory to soap and soap making. In 1790, by using salt, sulfuric acid, limestone, and coal to produce soda, Frenchman Nicholas Leblanc discovered a process of converting common salt to an alkali. He then extracted and crystallized the sodium carbonate. In scientific terms soap is a salt of a fatty acid. Due to the simplicity, this was the most popular method of making soap in the 19th century, although it used dangerous chemicals and produced a substantial amount of pollution. This led to the discovery of the ammonia-soda process in 1811 by Augustin Jean Fresenel. He combined ammonia with carbon dioxide to create bicarbonate soda, which was heated and mixed with fat to make soap. This method was very popular and is still used today. Other advancements in science and equipment contributed to the quality and consistency of soap.

Many chemical reactions take place when you make soap, by using a mixture of fats/oil, water and sodium hydroxide you can make amazing soaps. When you combine the fats/oil, water and sodium hydroxide you create a chemical reaction known as saponification. All of the ingredients in soap have very particular chemical characteristics that play an integral role in the soap making process. Fats and oils are triglycerides; triglycerides are 3 molecules of fatty acids attached to a single molecule of glycerol. The sodium hydroxide when mixed with water creates an alkaline solution. During saponification the triglycerides are hydrolyzed into free fatty acids, and then they combine with the alkaline solution to form an amalgam of salts, excess fat and glycerol. This chemical process makes soap. Glycerin is a by-product of the soap making process; many commercial manufactures remove the excess glycerin. When you make soap at home, either liquid soap or bar soap, your soap contains amounts of glycerin, making it beneficial to the skin. While it isn't necessary to understand the chemical reaction, you do have to be aware of it. Knowing how scientific the soap making process is makes its' discovery interesting and impressive.

Soaps, especially liquid soaps, should not be confused with detergents. While both soap and detergent can be used as surfactants: the term surfactant refers to the soap or detergents ability to break the surface tension of dirt and oil. Soap and detergent are made using different processes with different ingredients and different chemical reactions.

There are two methods to make liquid soap. One involves using premade bar soap that you melt and add water and other additives too. When you make soap this way you can use any type of soap that you like depending on why you want to make liquid soap. This method is very similar to milled soap. You melt the soap, but add enough water to make it a liquid. You can make your favorite bar soap into a liquid soap for easier use when bathing or to use as a bubble bath. You can also use castile soaps to make a liquid soap to serve as a base for just about any household or laundry soap you might need including dish soap, laundry soap, floor cleaner, abrasive cleanser, window cleaner and more. If you are making liquid soap just to try it out, you can use whatever soap is available. If you are making liquid soap because you want an all natural soap, then you will need to use an all natural soap to make the liquid soap and be sure that any additives you include are the same.

The other method involves taking raw ingredients, and making the liquid soap from scratch. The process involves combining oils with chemicals and then cooking them over heat before having to neutralize the soap. While there are many steps, making liquid soap is very achievable by any home crafter. If you've made cold process or hot process soap before you will be familiar with many of the steps, and will just have to add to the routine. If you have not made soap before, all you will need to do is to follow the recipe and the directions and you will be able to make a safe and gentle liquid soap for just about any purpose. Making liquid soap from premade soap is like making soup from a can, making liquid soap from scratch is like making soup from scratch. See what works best for you, just take your time and enjoy the experience.

By making liquid soaps you can remove many chemicals and synthetic products in your home. Many commercial liquid soaps such as shampoo, dish detergent, laundry detergent, pet shampoo and household cleaners are not soap, but detergent and contain harsh ingredients. You can create safe, fragrant and mild liquid soaps for yourself, your family and friends. You don't need specialty equipment to make liquid soap; you can find most everything you need to get started right in your home. As you continue to make liquid soap you will discover the tools and methods that work for you.

BENEFITS OF HOMEMADE LIQUID SOAP

Liquid soap is very sanitary to use and unlike bar soap is very tidy. Liquid soap is a very good way to cleanse the skin and remove dirt & bacteria. Liquid soap begins working as soon as it is dispensed. So you will spend less time trying to get the soap onto your hands and more time washing your hands. Liquid soaps can be made with emollient oils and pleasing scents, making them very enjoyable and relaxing for bathing.

If you are making liquid soap for household cleaning purposes you will not only save money, but ensure that your home is free of harsh ingredients and chemicals found in commercially produced cleaners, detergents and liquid soaps. You can use all natural nontoxic ingredients, to ensure you have a clean and safe living space.

Homemade liquid soap is very economical to use, both because of the costs related to making it and because there is little waste. It is very easy to control how much soap is used for any given purpose. Liquid soap is safe and effective for people of ages.

CHAPTER 2: LIQUID SOAP MAKING SAFETY

You will be implementing radically different safety procedures depending on how you are going to make liquid soap. If you are making liquid soap from previously made soap, the process is very straightforward. You will have to consider how you are going to melt the soap either with heat or with time. Using heat you can place the soap and water in the slow cooker (preferred method of melting as the heat is low and consistent) or with water and soak until the soap dissolves and becomes creamy with the water. If you use heat, you will want to make sure that the slow cooker is safely out of the reach of pets and children. Once the soap is melted you will have to take the proper safety measures depending on which additives you want to put in the soap. The melted soap itself is safe, but it will be hot, use proper gloves when handling the slow cooker. Be careful how you mix the soap. If you use an immersion blender to combine the additives place the blender into the soap with the end of the blender on the bottom of the pot, then turn the blender on, turn the blender off before removing it from the soap, this will reduce risks of the soap splattering. Even though the soap is not caustic it is hot and will irritate skin and eyes. Always wear safety glassed and insulated gloves.

Being aware of the properties of your additives is crucial. Many essential oils can be very irritating to skin and eyes at full strength. Essential oils are not even oils; they are highly concentrated botanical extracts. Make sure you wear safety glasses and gloves. If at any time you are splattered with hot soap or additives and experience irritation or pain, seek medical attention.

Liquid soap is made with lye or potassium hydroxide, also known as caustic potash. Potassium hydroxide is soluble than the lye used for bar soap, sodium hydroxide, the soluble potassium hydroxide makes liquid soap possible. Potassium hydroxide is safe to use, but you do have to use it properly. Always mix you potassium hydroxide and water in:

-A glass or non-reactive container
-In a well-ventilated area
-Always ADD the potassium hydroxide to the water, never the other way around.
-Always wear safety glasses and gloves when working the potassium hydroxide.

Potassium hydroxide is caustic, you can neutralize it with plain white vinegar, so always have a big bottle of white vinegar ready and available for use when you making liquid soap.

Once the potassium hydroxide is added to the water, stir it with a stainless steel spoon, until the potassium hydroxide dissolves. Combining the potassium hydroxide and water creates a chemical reaction, and the water gets very hot, often in excess of 200 degrees. This mixture will not cool the same way boiled water will, it can take hours to cool down. You will want to make sure you have you mixing jar clearly labeled and out of the reach of children and pets.

The liquid soap will have to undergo a lengthy saponification process which involves cooking the soap. The oils and fats will interact with the potassium hydroxide and water mixture and the temperature of the soap will be very high. Additionally the soap with be caustic until it is saponified. If you are making clear liquid soap, you will have to neutralize the soap to get rid of the extra lye and lower the pH. This can be done by boric acid, borax, or citric acid.

By implementing standard Safety Protocols you will ensure the safety and success of your liquid soap:
-Read the recipe thoroughly before you begin
-Have an uncluttered clean work space
-Have all your ingredients out and pre-measured
-Have all your tools and equipment cleaned and sanitized
-Wear safety glasses and gloves
-Have white vinegar available
-Be able to work without interruptions

CHAPTER 3: INSTRUCTIONS FOR LIQUID SOAP

EQUIPMENT REQUIRED

You don't need specialty equipment to make liquid soap. If you are making premade soap into liquid soap you can find most of the tools and equipment you need right in your own kitchen. Depending on the recipe you use, you may need to weigh ingredients, so a scale is helpful but not absolutely necessary. Depending on colorants or additives that you put into the soap you may want to use stainless steel bowls and measuring cups or spoons, so they don't stain or leave traces of fragrance.

To make liquid soap from premade soap you will need:

-Soap
-A grater or a sharp knife
-Water
-A large pot
-Optional: Additives (essential/fragrance oil or colorants)
-Empty soap dispensers

To make liquid soap from scratch you will need:
- Scale
- Measuring Cups
- Measuring Spoons
- Slow Cooker (recommended as it easier and safer)
- Wide Mouth Glass Jar
- Stainless Steel Spoon
- Immersion blender/blender
- Easy read thermometer
- Safety glass and Gloves
- White Vinegar
- Empty soap dispensers

For both methods of liquid soap making keep in mind the following tips. Make sure you use clean and sanitized equipment that is in good repair and is not chipped. Avoid using plastic, aluminum, tin or copper bowls or pans or Teflon coated pots. Use non-reactive bowls or pots to make your soap in. You can use heat resistant plastic to melt your oils (in the microwave) or for the potassium hydroxide/water solution, just make sure it can withstand temperatures in excess of 200 degree.

LIQUID SOAP MAKING INSTRUCTIONS

LIQUID SOAP FROM PRE-MADE SOAP BARS:

You can easily make liquid soap from premade soap bars by using the following method:

-Grate or chop up a 4 oz. bar of a soap of your choice .

-Bring four cups of distilled water to a boil.

-Remove water from heat and add the grated or cut up soap. Stir the soap until the soap is fully combined with the water.

-Let the soap and water mixture cool for several hours or overnight. You can check on it once and give it a good stir.

-After letting the mixture sit, check the consistency, if it is too thin, reheat and add more soap. If it is too thick add more water. For a very smooth soap you can mix it briefly in the blender or with the immersion blender. Too much mixing will make the soap bubble up. Consistency is a matter of preference based on what you like and what you intend to use the soap for.

-Once the consistency is where you want it, add some essential oil and coloring and place in dispensers, or save this base to use for another recipe.

LIQUID SOAP FROM SCRATCH:

-Read your recipe thoroughly.
-Gather all of your ingredients.
-Gather all of your clean and sanitized tools and equipment.
-Measure all of your ingredients.
-Wearing safety glasses and gloves add the lye to the water in a well-ventilated area.
-Melt the oils in the slow cooker on low.
-Once the lye is at the correct temperature add the lye solution to the oils.
-Blend the oil/lye mixture with the stick blender to combine them thoroughly.
-Continue blending until the soap is at the trace stage. Trace is when the soap is so thick it will hold an impression if you dip a spoon into it and pull it out. At this point you may want to replace the immersion blender with a spoon and cook the soap until it becomes a paste.
-Cook the paste for about 6 hours, stirring it approximately every 30 minutes. Do not leave the soap unattended while it is cooking. The paste is done when it dissolves clearly in boiling water. If the soap is white or cloudy in the water it isn't done, keep cooking and test again in 30 minutes.
-Once the paste is done, you will want to dilute it. Add measured distilled water as directed in the recipe. Many recipes will say that consistency is a matter of preference. It is always easier to err on the side of adding less water, as you can always add more, but removing water is more complicated.
-It can take the paste several hours to completely dissolve, do not leave the crock pot on overnight, as the diluted soap does not need to cook.
-Once the soap is dissolved and is the consistency you want, you can add essential or fragrance oils and colorants if you prefer.
-Store the soap in containers or save for use in another recipe.

CHAPTER 4: HOW TO ADD OTHER INGREDIENTS

There are many additives you can add to your liquid soap, depending on its' purpose. You can add items to suspend in hand soap for decoration, anti-bacterial essential oils for hand soap, abrasive items for a liquid body scrub soap or for a cleansing soap for household cleaning. Additives increase the soaps ability to perform the cleaning job it is meant to do. There really are no limits, you can be creative and have fun and make really beautiful products. You can add these when you are ready to place your liquid soap in its jar or bottle.

ADDING COLOR

When you add color to your liquid soap you must take into account the color of the soap base. Your soap base will take color characteristics from the oils that you have used to make it. If you used a tea infusion in your water, that too can affect the way the color will turn out. If you have an amber base and add blue to your soap it will appear more of a murky green than blue. This doesn't mean that you can't color your soap, it just means that have to think about how your colors will interact and color your soap according to the color in the base.

You can use pigments, water-soluble colorants, micas, clays, spice, tea or herbal infusions. Always make sure that your colorants are safe for topical use on the skin. If you are experimenting with teas or cocoa always test on fabric or do a patch test on your hand to check for staining. Soap supply stores sell a large variety of colorants that have been tested and are safe for use in liquid soap.

You can blend your colorant with a small amount of oil and then add it to your soap. Mixing the colorant in the oil will help it to not clump (if using powdered colorants) and to blend evenly and quickly in the soap. Blend the colorant thoroughly, scraping down the sides of the soap pot and scraping where the sides meet the bottom, to ensure an even color.

ADDING SCENT

The recipe you use will give you suggestions of types and amounts of essential oils or fragrance to use. You will want to know the properties of the fragrance oils and essential oils that you are using, as using to much of either can be irritating to the skin. Add the oil to the soap a few drops at a time and blend very well.

INGREDIENT SUGGESTIONS BASED ON SOAP TYPE

ESSENTIAL OILS FOR ANTI-BACTERIAL SOAP:

-Tea Tree Oil
-Lavender Essential Oil

FOR FACE WASH OR BODY SCRUB:

-Skin Oils, Vitamins
-Sugar
-Salt
-Ground Oatmeal

FOR HAND SCRUB:

-Coffee
-Cornmeal

FOR LIQUID HOUSEHOLD CLEANSERS & WINDOW SPRAY:

-Vinegar
-Baking Soda
-Essential Oils: Thyme, Rosemary, Lemon, Orange, Lavender, Eucalyptus

FOR ABRASIVE LIQUID SOAP CLEANSERS:

-Baking Soda
-Borax
-Salt
-Essential Oils: Orange, Lemon, Lavender, Thyme, Tea Tree

FOR LIQUID LAUNDRY SOAP:

-Borax
-Washing Soda
-Essential Oils: Lavender, Eucalyptus

CHAPTER 5: LIQUID SOAP RECIPES

Unless otherwise directed follow the directions for the Liquid Soap from Chapter 3.

SIMPLE LIQUID SOAP

-Lye & Water Solution: 11 oz. potassium hydroxide & 33 oz. distilled water
-24 oz. coconut oil
-10 oz. olive oil
-10 oz. castor oil
-3 oz. jojoba oil
-To neutralize: 3oz Borax & 6oz water heated until borax dissolves
-*Distilled Water to Consistency to dilute your soap

MOISTURIZING LIQUID SOAP

-Lye & Water Solution: 12oz potassium hydroxide & 36oz distilled water

-24oz soybean oil

-20oz coconut oil

-4oz Cocoa Butter

-To neutralize: 3oz Borax & 6oz water heated until borax dissolves

-*Distilled Water to Consistency to dilute your soap

LIQUID CASTILE SOAP

-Lye & Water Solution: 9.25 oz. potassium hydroxide & 33 0z. distilled water.
-47 oz. olive oil
-To neutralize: 3oz Borax & 6oz water heated until borax dissolves
-*Distilled Water to Consistency to dilute your soap

LIQUID HAND SOAP

-1 bar unscented soap, grated
-3 quarts water
-1 tsp essential oil
-Bring water and soap to a boil, stir well. Allow mixture to sit and stir frequently, adjust consistency as needed. Add essential oil, transfer liquid soap to pump dispensers.

GREASE CUTTING LIQUID HAND SOAP

-1 bar unscented soap, grated
-3 quarts water
-1 cup ground pumice or cornmeal
-½ tsp tea tree oil
-½ teaspoon lavender oils
-½ teaspoon orange oil
-Bring water and soap to a boil, stir well. Allow to sit and stir frequently, adjust consistency as needed. Add other ingredients, transfer liquid soap to pump dispensers.

LIQUID SHAMPOO

- ¼ cup coconut milk
- ¼ Cup distilled water or tea infusion
- 1/3 cup castile soap
- 1 teaspoon vitamin e
- 20 drops of your favorite essential oil
- 1/2 teaspoon olive oil

-Combine all ingredients in a bowl and stir well to combine, for use transfer to a foaming dispenser. Shake well before use, keeps for up to 30 days.

LIQUID SHAVING SOAP

-¼ cup honey
-¼ cup distilled water or tea infusion
-1/3 cup castile soap
-1 teaspoon vitamin e
-20 drops of mint or eucalyptus essential oil
-1 teaspoon olive oil
-Combine all ingredients in a bowl and stir well to combine, for use transfer to a foaming dispenser. Shake well before use, keeps for up to 30 days.

MOISTURIZING LIQUID BODY SOAP

-⅔ cup liquid castile soap
-¼ cup honey
-2 teaspoons sweet almond oil
-1 teaspoon vitamin e
-30 drops of favorite essential oil or blend of essential oils

SIMPLE LIQUID LAUNDRY SOAP

-14 oz. Bar of Soap*, grated
-1/2 Cup Borax
-3/4 Cup Washing Soda
-12 Cups Boiling Water
-Combine all ingredients in a 5 gallon bucket and allow mixture to sit for 24 hours, Fill the bucket to the top with hot water and blend with immersion blender. Your liquid laundry soap is ready to use. * Fels Naptha or Zote are popular soaps available in the supermarket for liquid laundry soap. Use ¼ Cup per load.

LIQUID DISHWASHER SOAP

-3 cups of very hot water
-1 ¼ cups washing soda
-3 tablespoons liquid castile soap
-Combine all ingredients in a 1 quart glass jar, stir well until everything is incorporated. Use 1 ½ tablespoons per load.

ALL PURPOSE SPRAY CLEANSER

-1 gallon very hot water
-1 Tablespoon baking soda
-2 teaspoons liquid castile soap
-2 teaspoons preferred essential oil
-Combine all ingredients and mix very well, pour into spray bottles. Shake well before using.

LIQUID TUB AND TOILET BOWL CLEANSER

-1 cup liquid castile soap
-2 cups borax
-1 cup water
-1 teaspoon tea tree oil
-Combine all ingredients mixing very well, place in a squeeze bottle or jar. Apply to toilet or tub with a brush or towel, wait 15 minutes and rinse.

ALL PURPOSE ABRASIVE SOAP CLEANSER

-1 cup baking soda
-¼ cup liquid castile soap
-½ cup water
-1 teaspoon orange essential oil
-Combine all ingredients mixing very well, place in a squeeze bottle or jar. Apply to surface with a brush or towel, wait 15 minutes and rinse.

HARDWOOD, TILE AND LINOLEUM FLOOR SOAP

-1 gallon water
-1/4 cup liquid castile soap
-1/8 cup white distilled vinegar
-1 teaspoon essential oil of choice
-Combine all ingredients and mix very well, pour into spray bottles. Shake well before using. Spray onto surface and mop vigorously with a damp mop.

WOOD FURNITURE SOAP CLEANSER

-2 teaspoons olive oil
-1 cup lemon juice
-3 cups water
-1 Tablespoon liquid castile soap
-2 tablespoon orange essential oil
-Combine all ingredients and mix very well, pour into spray bottles. Shake well before using. Spray onto surface and polish vigorously with a lint free towel.

SPRAY WINDOW SOAP CLEANER

-2 cups distilled water
-1/4 cup white vinegar
-1/2 teaspoon castile liquid soap
-Combine all ingredients and mix very well, pour into spray bottles. Shake well before using. Spray onto surface and polish vigorously with a lint free towel.

FRUIT AND VEGETABLE WASH

- ¼ teaspoon liquid castile soap
- 1 tablespoon lemon juice
- 2 tablespoons baking soda
- 1 cup water
- Combine all ingredients and mix very well, pour into spray bottles. Shake well before using. Spray on vegetables and then rinse them in cold water.

CHAPTER 6: HOW TO CREATE RECIPES

After you've made a few liquid soap recipes and have learned how to make liquid soap you can start to create your own recipes. You can create recipes based on the ingredients that are easy to find in your area, or using ingredients that you order from a soap making supply store. There are many online resources to help you when you make your own recipes. You will always need to use a lye calculator to determine how much lye/water you need to saponify the fats/oils you use. Remember that you use potassium hydroxide to make liquid soap, many soap calculators have a default setting for bar soap, so make sure you enter in the correct data.

Creating your own recipes is very fun and the possibilities are endless. The most fun part of making liquid soap is how you can use the soap in so many creative and useful ways. One batch of liquid castile soap can make enough household cleaning products to last a very long time. By mixing different fragrance or essential oils you can create bubble baths and soaps for use in aromatherapy.

When you begin creating your own recipes you will want to start out by selecting the base oils you want to use in your liquid soap. The properties of your base oils will affect the clarity, quality, texture and lather of your finished liquid soap. You can use olive oil by itself to create the classic castile soap, which can be used for anything and everything. You can also mix and match oils and fats to create creamy lather, lots of bubbles and moisturizing benefits. It all depends on the intended use of your finished liquid soap.

You will use a lye calculator to determine how much potassium hydroxide and water (or other liquid) to use. Have your recipe written down, you will need to know the types of oils and the weights that you want to use. You will be given an amount of water for the potassium hydroxide and lye solution, but you will have to use your judgment on how much water to add to make the liquid soap the consistency that you would like. Many recipes will give you a range and you will start to have an idea of this yourself as you make more liquid soap.

Many calculators will give you a % of excess fat and a percentage to superfat. If you have 0% of excess fat, you will need to superfat. During saponification the moisturizing properties of your oils and fats is cancelled out by the chemical reaction of the lye. By superfatting the soap you will ensure that your soap is creamy and moisturizing to the skin, not drying. You can also add extra oils, nutrients, botanicals and additives if you make a liquid soap base to use in other recipes.

CHAPTER 7: HOW TO PACKAGE AND LABEL LIQUID SOAP

There are many styles and shapes of containers you can use to package your liquid soap. You can use simple glass jars, recycle other containers that have had liquid soap products in them, or buy new containers.

Chose an appropriate container for the type of soap you have. Liquid hand soap can be put in a bottle with a pump dispenser or a foaming dispenser, liquid dish soap can be put in a squirt bottle, body wash in a squirt bottle, face cleanser in a pump dispenser, all purpose cleaner and window cleaner in a spray bottle. Cleaning is hard enough, so make the best decision for ease of use with the cleaning products that you make. Always clearly label and date the products you make, so you and everyone else will know what they contain and how they should be used.

If you want to sell your products, you can use store bought containers or have people bring their own containers. You will need to create labels for your product. Soap labeling laws are quite straightforward. Soaps are products made with oil and lye, soap products cannot make any cosmetic claims such as; deodorizing, moisturizing, nourishing, etc. Labeling laws for soap are regulated in the United States by the FDA. Products made from pre made bars fall under this labeling regulation as long as the pre made bar was soap made from oil and lye not commercial detergent. Homemade liquid soap is considered soap and as long as you follow the guidelines you can sell your soap. The following items are suggested items for your soap labels:

-You will want to identify your product as soap: ie. abrasive cleansing soap, hand soap, etc.
-Weight or volume of the soap
-Your business name and address
-List of the ingredients, in descending order of the most used to the least. You will want to write the common names of the ingredients. You can either write the names of the raw ingredients, or you write the names of the

ingredients after they have changed during the chemical reaction and saponification process. You do not have to list ingredients that are 1% or less of the recipe, and you do not have to specify the type of fragrance, but can just write 'fragrance'.

Your labels can be reflective of your style and the volume of your business. If you are making gifts for family and friends, a handwritten label is personal and gives the receiver all of the information they need. If you plan on selling large volumes of liquid soap handwritten labels may not be realistic. There are many software programs that can help you make fun and professional looking labels for your products.

CHAPTER 8: LIQUID SOAPMAKING FAQ'S

CAN YOU MAKE LIQUID SOAP WITHOUT POTASSIUM HYDROXIDE?

-Liquid soap from scratch cannot be made without potassium hydroxide. Potassium hydroxide is perfectly safe to use at home with the proper safety precautions. Potassium hydroxide when combined with water, creates a chemical reaction that binds oils and fats in a process called saponification. When you follow a liquid soap recipe using the correct amounts of all ingredients and adhere to the safety protocols, your homemade liquid soap with be gentler and milder than any commercially made soap you can buy at the store. However, by using premade bar soap you can make liquid soap at home without having to use potassium hydroxide.

CAN I RECYCLE SOAP SCRAPS?

-Yes. You can recycle all of your soap scraps ones from your homemade soap and even add in store bought scarps or bars. Grate the soap or cut it up into small pieces, you can melt the soap in a slow cooker with water. Add enough water to make a thin liquid when all of the soap is melted. For a medium consistency liquid soap plan on using 3-4 cups of water per 4 oz. of bar soap. You can add any additives that you like including essential oils, fragrance, exfoliants, botanicals and extra fats or oils. Allow the soap to cool before transferring it to a container.

I'M CONFUSED BY ALL THE STEPS, CAN I MAKE LIQUID SOAP?

-Yes. If you can work undisturbed and can focus on making, you will be just fine. Start out by making liquid soap from premade bar soap. From there you can gain confidence and try making liquid soap from scratch. Follow the directions in the instructions chapter and any additional instructions in the recipe.

HOW LONG WILL MY HOMEMADE LIQUID SOAP LAST?

-Home made liquid soap will last a very long time when made and stored correctly. You need to use a good recipe and follow the directions, making sure you measure every ingredient correctly. If you follow the recipe using correct proportions and store the soap in a clean dry area, it can be stored for years. For soap stored for an excessively long time or stored under extreme conditions (like extreme heat or cold) you may notice a decrease in the aroma or a fading of the color, or the soap may dry and harden, however you can re-batch it with water and bring it back to the consistency that you like.

TIPS TO HELP IMPROVE YOUR SOAPS' SHELF LIFE:
-Follow the recipe.
-Use quality oils.
-Don't put too many additives in your soap; ie fruits, plants, vegetables, herbs, or flour.
-Package your soap in modest size containers.
-Clearly label and date your soap.

IS MY LIQUID SOAP ALL NATURAL OR ORGANIC?
-Your liquid soap can be all natural or organic, depending on the ingredients you chose to use. Many ingredients claim they are natural or organic, make sure they have the proper documentation to back up that claim when you purchase them.

WHEN CAN I ADD FRAGRANCE AND COLOR TO THE SOAP?
-Once the soap is neutralized it's time to add fragrance and color. Many recipes will list an amount of colorant, essential oil or fragrance to use. Measuring the amounts is important as using too much color or scent can be irritating to the skin.

SHOULD I USE FRAGRANCE OILS OR ESSENTIAL OILS IN MY SOAP?
-You can use either or both. Many fragrance oils are blends of all natural oils although some contain synthetic fragrances. Fragrance oils have been stabilized so the aroma will last longer than essential oils. Essential oils often contain many beneficial properties that are good for the skin and the

senses. Use products that you like and that make your soap smell the way you want it to.

CHAPTER 9: ALLERGY CONSIDERATIONS

Many people are affected by allergies, knowing the ingredients you use in your soap will help you to avoid triggering an allergic reaction in anyone that uses the liquid soap you make. People with allergies and sensitivities are very aware and conscientious of the products they use on their skin and in their homes. As homemade liquid soap uses natural oils and ingredients it is milder and gentle on the skin and senses.

Many commercially made cleaning soaps are actually detergents and are made with synthetic ingredients and fragrances that can irritate skin and trigger allergic reactions. Keeping your ingredients simple and natural is a good idea.

By combing your safe, gentle and mild liquid soap base with additives to make personal and household cleaning liquid soap, you will be able to create many different kinds of liquid soaps to meet all of your cleaning needs.

DISCLAIMER

This book about Making Liquid is intended for entertainment purposes only. It is not intended to be and should not be taken as instruction for the craft of liquid soap making. You should seek professional hands on instructional classes in Liquid Soap Making if you have any questions or concerns.

While it is perfectly safe is used properly potassium hydroxide is a serious chemical. You will need to follow safety protocols by wearing safety glasses, safety gloves, using the proper equipment, work in a well-ventilated area and always adding the potassium hydroxide to the water. By adhering to the safety protocols you reduce risks associated with using potassium hydroxide. Potassium hydroxide is very caustic until it has saponified with the oils and been neutralized. Should potassium hydroxide come in contact with your skin it can easily be neutralized with white vinegar. Seek medical attention as it is appropriate for you. Always keep children and pets away from the work are and the potassium hydroxide solution. Always clearly label the all of your making tools, equipment, ingredients and solutions. Keep the potassium hydroxide stored in a safe area away from the reach of children and pets.

When heating oils, always use low heat and closely monitor the melting process. Do not leave the oils unattended on the stovetop or in the microwave. The oils only need to be warmed enough to melt. Keep children and pets away from work area and the heated oils.

While I have tested the recipes included in this book and have made them successfully, I cannot guarantee how they will turn out for you. I do not know the quality of the ingredients that you will be using, the type of equipment you have available or your skill level. Always measure and weigh your ingredients, take your time and work undisturbed if possible.

Liquid soap making is a creative and rewarding craft. I hope you enjoy making many wonderful liquid soap recipes I've included for years to come using both of the methods mentioned in this book.

Book 3: "Homemade Body Butter & Lotion For Beginners"

CHAPTER 1: HISTORY OF LOTION & BODY BUTTER

Today there are literally thousands of different lotions, each targeted for specific skin types and purposes – anti-wrinkle, oil-free, extra moisturizing and sensitive, just to name a few. Many lotions contain retinols, alpha & beta-hydroxy acids, vitamins and minerals and are blended with vegetable and plant ingredients. Most lotions are formulated to smooth, hydrate and soften the skin; some lotions are used as a medicine delivery system. But lotion hasn't always been fancy or complicated.

The concept of lotion has been around longer than the wheel. Moisturizer has been in use dating back to 8000 BC. To put that in perspective, the wheel was invented in approximately 3500BC. Depending on where a person was living and what types of oils and fats were available, determined what types of lotions were made to soothe and hydrate the skin. In Latin America people used avocado oil, in Brazil and Africa people used palm oil and Native Americans used animal fat. Ancient history is full of romantic tales of scented moisturizing oils. Homer told the tale of Queen Hera using scented Olive Oil to seduce the God Zeus. Cleopatra was notorious for her use of scented olive and sesame oils.

Overtime cosmetic scientists have developed recipes that blended oils with scents and water that promote good skin health. By using an emulsifying agent they could create a creamy lotion, as preservatives were discovered the lotion became shelf stable. After the Industrial revolution synthetic ingredients such as petroleum jelly and mineral oil became standard ingredients in lotions. The science of skin care continues to evolve as advancements are made in understanding how the skin absorbs nutrients and moisture.

The appearance and feel of skin is essential to inter personal attraction and interaction. While lotions are topically applied, the beneficial effects on the whole person are profound. If your skin has been exposed to harsh environmental conditions such as ultraviolet light, environmental and occupational factors using lotion is part of healing and protecting your skin. A good lotion made of quality ingredients supports the skin's mechanism for maintaining optimum water content.

Skin that is well hydrated is softer and supple. Having well hydrated and protected skin is the primary objective of a good skin care routine.

CHAPTER 2: DIFFERENT TYPES OF LOTIONS

Lotion is simply oil and water that is emulsified together. Most commercially made lotions contain large amounts of water and trace amounts of ingredients that nourish and moisturize your skin. Commercially made lotions are made using industrial strength emulsifiers and stabilizers so they can hold the maximum amount of water and be shelf stable for years.

You can make amazing lotions and creams for yourself, your family and your friends for fractions of what you can spend buying lotions and creams at the store. Why pay expensive prices for something you can make yourself? You can create beautiful lotions and cream in minutes in your very own kitchen.

There are many different types of lotions that you can make. A typical lotion is a lightweight blend of oils and water. Creams usually contain less water and are of a thicker consistency. Lotion bars and body butters are usually oils bound together with an emulsifying agent such as beeswax or emulsifying wax. Lotion bars are usually more solid.

You can also make lotions for specific purposes. You can make face lotions containing botanicals and skin nutrients, hand lotions with extra moisturizing ingredients and lotions for the whole body.

Homemade lotions contain rich hydrating ingredients to protect the skin. Using the oils from nuts, seeds, vegetables and fruit from around the world, your lotions will have many beneficial fatty acids and anti-oxidants. Using all natural oils will ensure that you can make smooth and creamy lotions. Lotion creates a protective barrier on the skins surface and allows the skin to hydrate. The protective barrier created by lotions and creams protects skin from harsh elements, such as heating, sun, air conditioning and wind.

HOW MOISTURIZERS WORK TO PROTECT THE SKIN:

Each ingredient in your lotion has a specific purpose not only in creating the emulsification but also in protecting, nourishing and moisturizing the skin.

-Humectants: Attract water to your skin

-Emollients: Oils that hydrate your skin

-Barrier: Protects the skin and lets the skin absorb nutrients and moisture.

-Emulsifier & Thickener: Holds the water and oil together in a consistent state. Allows the lotion or cream to be applied easily.

-Preservative: Prevents bacteria from growing in the lotion and ensures the lotion is safe for your skin.

LOTIONS FOR DIFFERENT SKIN TYPES

Lotions moisturize to prevent and heal skin problems such as: oiliness, dryness or sensitivity. Lotions protect sensitive skin while improving skin tone and texture. Skin that is not rehydrated and moisturized can become so dry it can harden into painful callouses and crack, causing pain and discomfort. Dry skin can be uncomfortable and more prone to infection if scratched. Skin that is properly hydrated and protected stays soft and supple, and is resilient and able to withstand normal environmental conditions.

NORMAL SKIN

Lotions can prevent normal skin form becoming too oily or too dry. Normal skin can be rehydrated with lightweight water based moisturizers.

DRY SKIN

Lotions can heal dry skin and make it soft and supple. Dry skin can be rehydrated and moisturized with thick lotions or creams that help protect and heal the skin by preventing water evaporation.

OILY SKIN

Lotions can rehydrate oily skin after bathing or after being exposed to sun and wind. Using light water based moisturizers is best for oily skin.

AGING SKIN

Lotions that are rich and creamy work the best for aging skin. Using botanicals and vitamins that have anti-oxidant and anti-wrinkle properties helps aging skin stay soft and well hydrated.

SENSITIVE SKIN

Sensitive skin is more vulnerable to skin irritations, rashes, redness or itching. Lotions that contain soothing botanicals such as aloe, calendula and chamomile help soothe and repair sensitive skin. Avoid using dyes or synthetic fragrances in lotions for sensitive skin.

ECZEMA

Eczema is best treated with thicker very emollient lotions such as a lotion bar. Adding tea tree oil helps soothe and relieve pain and irritation due to eczema.

CHAPTER 3: SAFETY & SANITATION PROCEDURES

Lotion is very safe to make. You do however need to practice safety procedures as the oils can burn if left unattended and some of the concentrated ingredients can irritate the skin and the eyes.

When heating the oils be very careful. Always use a heavy bottomed pot or large glass bowl. Do not leave the oils unattended. If you melt your oils in the microwave, be sure that you check on them every 30-45 seconds. If you melt your oils on the stove top keep the heat on low and stir the oils checking on them every 30-45 seconds. Once oil gets hot, it retains heat very well and can become exponentially hotter. If you leave the oils unattended you risk the oils boiling over and creating a burn hazard and a fire risk. Always use padded oven gloves when handling the oil pot or bowl.

You need to be very aware of the ingredients you are using. Knowing how to properly handle and use your ingredients will make your lotion making safer and more enjoyable. Many of the ingredients in lotion are very concentrated and can be irritating to the skin if applied at 100% potency. Essential oils are not actually oils, they are concentrated plant extracts. While the compounds in essential oils are very beneficial to the skin, they must be diluted for safe use. Wear gloves and protective eyewear anytime you measure, combine and mix ingredients into a lotion.

Before you begin make sure you have a clean uncluttered workspace. Having plenty of room to make your lotion and having you ingredients, equipment and tools laid out will be more efficient. Always read your recipe and pre measure all of your ingredients.

The most important part of making lotion safely is to make sure that everything is clean and sanitized. You will be using a preservative in your lotion, but you want to avoid introducing bacteria into your lotion. As most people make lotion in their kitchens, sanitizing the workspace, tools and equipment will prevent any cross-contamination from potentially hazardous foods in your kitchen.

You can use soap and hot water to clean everything and then a sanitizing solution to sanitize your equipment and tools. You can use a simple bleach solution by mixing 1 Tablespoon of bleach to 1 gallon of water. Allow jars, and tools to soak in the solution for at least 1 minute and then allow them to air-dry completely. If you follow the directions for using bleach it is very safe and effective, or you can use sanitizers made for crafting lotions. You can also use 70% isopropyl alcohol, 70% works better than 100%, as the water in the solution denatures the proteins in bacteria. Craft and lotion suppliers do sell sanitizing mixes and they also work very well.

EQUIPMENT REQUIRED

You don't need any fancy or specialty equipment to make lotion. You can make lotion with simple equipment and tools found in your kitchen. Always make sure your equipment is non-reactive and safe to use on the stovetop or in the microwave.

Basic equipment for creams and lotions:

-Immersion Blender: To combine the ingredients into a smooth emulsification.

-Scale: to accurately and correctly weigh your ingredients.

-Glass or Stainless Steel Bowls: to melt and mix your ingredients in

-Thermometer: for testing the temperature of oils

-Rubber Spatula: for getting all of the lotion or cream out of the mixing bowl

-Lightweight plastic bowls to weigh ingredients in

-Containers to put your lotions and cream in

Having a good quality scale will help you to get good results when making lotion. Many lotion recipes are written using the metric measuring system, so having a digital scale that can weigh in grams is very useful and you won't have to convert the measurement to ounces. If you do have to convert from metric to standard it is very useful to know that there are 28.3495 grams (g) in an ounce, 453.592 grams in 1 pound and 1000 grams in 1 kilogram. For liquid volume measurements in milliliters/ml 100g of water is the same as 100ml of water. However, this isn't accurate for all liquids – oil weighs less than water so 100g of oil might only measure 80ml.

Depending on the size of your recipe, many of the additives you are using will be in very small amounts, so having a scale that can weigh in 0.1-gram increments is very useful. When you are using essential oils and other ingredients with anti-aging and anti-oxidant properties you want to be very accurate in your measurements, as those ingredients are very potent and can be irritating to the skin if too much is used. If you do not have access to a scale, you can make a volume conversion 1 milliliter is approximately equal to 20 drops.

CHAPTER 4: UNDERSTANDING THE INGREDIENTS

Lotion is an emulsified blend of oil and water. You can use lanolin, beeswax or an emulsifying wax to bind the ingredients together. When you make lotions there are two ways to think of the emulsification, as oil in water or as water in oil. An oil in water emulsification means that you have small droplets of oil in a medium of water. A water in oil emulsification means that you have small droplets of water in a medium of oil. This simply expresses the ratio of water to oil.

Depending on the type of lotion/cream/body-butter/balm you want, you can use different ratios of oil to water, water to oil or oil to oil. When making lotions or creams the first ingredients will always be oil and water. You can also add vitamins, skin nutrients, essential oils and botanicals to your lotion to support healthy skin.

OILS

Oils create a barrier that holds moisture and allows the skin to hydrate and absorb nutrients and botanicals. Chose your oils according to the feel you want for your lotion or cream. Avocado, hemp, jojoba, grape-seed, apricot kernel, peach kernel, sweet almond, coconut, sesame, and olive oil are all good choices. By combining different oils you can create very emollient lotions that protect and hydrate the skin. You can also add plant and seed butters: shea, cocoa and mango.

WATER

Use pure distilled water if possible. If you can't use distilled water, boil your water actively for at least 5 minutes to sanitize it, allow the water to cool before using. Your skin will absorb the moisture in the water, so using clean sanitized water is very important. You can infuse the water with teas, and herbs. You can also buy extracts of many botanicals but you can also make infusions at home very simply. If you make an infusion, the color of the water will affect the color of your lotion. Some teas can stain clothing and skin, so be careful with which teas you use. If you have any concerns you can always do a simple test with a small cloth and a small area of skin. You can also use pure natural aloe vera gel in place of some or all of the water. Aloe vera has amazing skin nourishing properties and will add more body to your lotion.

EMULSIFIERS

Oil and water cannot mix and stay suspended together on their own. Water and oil need an emulsifying agent. The emulsifying agent helps bind the water and the oil together so it will not separate. Emulsifiers work because they have hydrophilic lipophilic balance (HLB) properties. It is important that you understand the HLB properties of the emulsifying agent that you are working with. Emulsifiers with low HLBs, such as lanolin or beeswax are good for water in oil lotions. Emulsifiers with higher HLBs like emulsifying wax, work best for oil in water lotions.

THICKENERS

Thickeners can be added to change the texture and spread-ability of your lotion. Many lotion supply stores sell thickeners such as xanthium-gum, hydrolyzed silk and modified starches. These thickeners reduce the heaviness and oiliness of oils and waxes.

VITAMINS, NUTRIENTS AND ANTI-OXIDANTS

There are many vitamins, nutrients and anti-oxidants you can add to your lotion. You can add nutrients and additives that you have tried before or experiment with new ones. You can order specialty skin nutrients from lotion supply stores; however, many vitamins and essential oils are available at your local pharmacy.

PRESERVATIVES

Adding preservatives will help your lotion last longer. Oils can turn rancid when exposed to varying temperatures, light and air. Water can grow bacteria, mold and yeasts. Vitamin E is an excellent preservative and also provides nourishment to the skin. Use -Germall Plus (0.1% to 0.5 % of the total formula) **OR** Otiphen Plus (0.75% to 1.5% of the total formula) and add it the oil before combining it with the water and emulsifying agent.

This will ensure that it is properly disbursed. These preservatives can be easily found online or at a lotion supply store.

CHAPTER 5: ADDITIVES
COLOR AND SCENTS

COLOR

Because colorants can stain skin and clothing, you must be careful when adding colorants to lotion. Colorants can irritate skin and cause allergic reactions. Always use water-soluble colorants that are cosmetic or food grade. You can use micas as well. Many oil-soluble oxides and pigments do not disburse well in lotions and can be streaky on the skin.

Always use colors that state that they are safe for use on the skin and body. You can always patch test fabric to see if it will stain.

You can make infusions of plants and botanicals either in oil or water, which will color your lotion, as well as add aroma and healing properties. You can make an infusion with water and botanicals by gently boiling the water with herbs, spices or roots. You can make an infusion with oil and botanicals by blending the oil with the ingredient and letting it steep for several days or a week, then straining out the ingredients.

If you want to make sunless tanning lotions or creams, you can make an infusion using dried green tea and dried linden flowers, you can also use black tea, coffee and cocoa powder. These ingredients are safe and all natural. You can adjust how potent the color is depending on skin tone and what shade of 'sun-less tan' you want.

Natural sunscreens can be made by adding titanium oxide or zinc oxide. Some oils like coconut and shea butter naturally have a SPF of 4. Zinc oxide will make your lotion an opaque white and can be a nice base for adding other colors and make the color of your lotion more vibrant.

SCENT

There are many ways to add lovely scents to your lotions. Some of the oils that you use will have a very light, sweet natural fragrance. Depending on the type of lotion and its' intended purpose you can scent your lotion however you wish. You can use any of the following to safely add scent to your creations:

-Teas/Tisanes
-Cocoa or Coffee
-Essential Oils
-Herbal or Fruit Infusions
-Fragrance Oils

OILS & OTHER ADDITIVES

Aloe Vera Gel

Aloe Vera has been used traditionally to treat skin conditions, including psoriasis, eczema, inflammation, burns and wounds. Aloe is a great skin hydrator; it brings oxygen to the cells, increasing the strength of skin tissue. Aloe has an effective penetrating ability that helps transport healthy substances through the skin.

Sesame Oil

Sesame oil is well known for its' amazing moisturizing qualities. Sesame oil has a SPF factor of 3-4, and helps regrow cells.

Coconut Oil

Coconut oil improves the moisture and lipid content of skin; it is especially good for very dry flaky skin. Coconut oil has powerful anti-microbial properties and can kill bacteria, viruses and fungi. Coconut oil also has a SPF of 4-5.

Olive Oil

Olive oil is a well-known remedy for very dry skin. It's silky smooth and does not usually cause allergic reactions, making it great oil for all skin types.

Mango Butter

This highly prized butter is from the seed kernel of the Mango tree. Mango Butter has very emollient moisturizing properties and is a lubricant for the skin.

Cocoa Butter

Cocoa butter is an aromatic solid butter pressed from the seeds of the Cacao tree. It has a very soft light brown color and a sweet rich aroma. Cocoa butter acts as a skin protectant and makes lotions very creamy. Cocoa butter helps skin heal and is most commonly used for stretch marks.

Shea Butter

Shea butter comes from the Karite Tree. Shea butter forms a breathable, water-resistant layer on the skin. Shea butter encourages hydration and healing.

Avocado Oil

Avocado oil contains high amounts of Vitamin A, B1, B2, D, and E. Avocado oil is especially helpful for skin problems such as eczema and psoriasis. It can be used on sensitive skin and problem skin that needs vitamin rich oil.

Almond Oil

Almond oil is great for all skin types. It is an amazing emollient that will soothe, soften, and re-condition the skin. Very rich in fatty acids, almond oil is also a shelf stable carrier oil.

Beeswax

Beeswax is an incredible substance made by worker honeybees. Beeswax is very fragrant and gives body and texture to lotions; it also acts as an emulsifying agent for oils and water.

Emulsifying Wax

Emulsifying waxes are typically vegetable bases waxes that act as an emulsifying agent for oils and water. They are typically allergen and scent free.

Lanolin

Lanolin is made by sheep, it protects and absorbs into skin. Capable of holding up to 400 times its weight in water, it's a fantastic moisture reservoir for hydration. Lanolin acts as an emulsifying for oils and water as well.

Vitamin E

Vitamin E is an antioxidant that helps protect cell membranes. It also reduces the effects of pollutants and nourishes dry skin. Because of it's powerful antioxidant properties it is a good preservative to use in lotions.

ESSENTIAL OILS AND PLANT EXTRACTS

Tea Tree Oil

Tea tree oil is the essential oil derived from the Australian native plant *Melaleuca Alternifolia*. Well known for its antimicrobial properties, tea tree oil is especially useful for problem skin and for healing skin.

Peppermint

The refreshing and invigorating aroma of peppermint does more than lift your spirits. Mint has mild astringent and exfoliating properties. Mint reduces inflammation and loosens dead skin cells, making it very good for oily or problem skin.

Lavender

Lavender essential oil has anti-microbial properties and is good for problem skin, yet is gentle enough for sensitive skin. Lavender is most well known for it's wonderful aroma that induces relaxation and reduces stress.

Rose

Rose essential oil has an amazingly sweet and fragrant aroma and is well known for improving the look and health of all skin types.

Geranium

Geranium is well known for its astringent and anti-inflammatory properties. Geranium oil is very refreshing and especially useful in treating problem and oily skin. It can also help diminish the appearance of lines and wrinkles.

Rosemary

Rosemary essential oil is noted for its ability to treat many skin conditions such as acne, dermatitis and eczema. Rosemary oil reduces swelling and puffiness and promotes healthy cell turn over.

Carrot Seed

Carrot seed essential oil is one of super star essential oils for healthy skin. Carrot seed oil rejuvenates and stimulates the skin, encouraging elasticity. It is also good for skin problems such as psoriasis and eczema.

Eucalyptus

Eucalyptus oil is well known for its' refreshing and relaxing aroma, but it is also great for problem skin. Due to its' antiseptic properties it will soothe heal painful skin eruptions and infections.

Arnica Montana

Traditionally Arnica Montana has been used externally to heal wounds, prevent bruising and swelling after injuries. Arnica reduces inflammation and pain. It can be used to help treat fungal and bacterial infections. Arnica is also used to treat insect bites and burns, including sunburn.

Comfrey Leaf

Comfrey has antibacterial, antifungal and anti-inflammatory properties. It is an effective remedy for many skin conditions. It reduces swelling and inflammation, relieves pain and stimulates cell growth. Comfrey contains vitamins A, C and B Complex vitamins including B12.

Yarrow Extract

Yarrow has anti-inflammatory and pain relieving properties. It repairs damaged tissues, reduces stretch marks. Yarrow has astringent properties making it good for oily or problem skin.

Chamomile Extract

Chamomile reduces puffiness and cleans oil and dirt from pores. It softens and soothes skin, and reduces dark eye circles. Chamomile has exceptional healing properties and is very good for skin irritations and sensitive skin.

CHAPTER 6: HOW TO MAKE LOTION, BODY BUTTER & CREAMS

Lotion is very simple to make. In just a few minutes you can make a soothing, regenerating lotion to heal and repair your skin. You can use the best ingredients; organic oils, pure water, essential oils, botanicals and skin nourishing vitamins. You can make lotions to moisturize, nourish or that have a medicinal use. Your skin will look and feel amazing when you use a very high quality product that you made yourself.

HOW TO MAKE LOTION

You will begin making Lotion by:
-Cleaning and sanitizing your workspace
-Cleaning and sanitizing your equipment, tools and containers
-Gathering all of your ingredients
-Measuring all of your ingredients
-Melting your oils
-Melting your emulsifying agent or wax
-Heating your water*
-Combine all of your ingredients in one mixing container
-Using the immersion blender, blend the lotion**
-Pour the lotion into containers
-Allow the lotion to cool, then date and label
-Clean up and put away your equipment and tools.

*Measure the temperature of both the oils and the emulsifying agent or wax, heat your water to that temperature. You only need to melt the oils and waxes to a liquid state.

*Place the immersion blender into the mixing bowl on the bottom of the bowl, turn the blender on and slowly move it around in a circular fashion. Do not plunge the immersion blender up and down, as this could cause the lotion to splatter. Be careful to not over mix the lotion, overmixing will introduce air into the lotion, which you do not want to do.

HOW TO MAKE BODY BUTTER

You will begin making Body Butter by:
-Cleaning and sanitizing your workspace
-Cleaning and sanitizing your equipment, tools and containers
-Gathering all of your ingredients
-Measuring all of your ingredients
-Melt your ingredients together in a double boiler.
-Using the immersion blender, blend the body butter.
-Allow the mixture to cool, refrigerate for an hour or two.
-Using a stand or hand mixer, beat the mixture until it is light and fluffy.
-Add essential oils or botanicals and beat to incorporate.
-Place the body butter into containers
-Date and label the body butter
-Clean up and put away your equipment and tools.

HOW TO MAKE LOTION BARS, SALVES OR BALMS

You will begin making lotion bars, salves or balms by:
- Cleaning and sanitizing your workspace
- Cleaning and sanitizing your equipment, tools and containers
- Gathering all of your ingredients
- Measuring all of your ingredients
- Melt your ingredients together in a double boiler
- Add essential oils or botanicals
- Using the immersion blender, blend the mixture on the lowest setting
- Place the mixture into containers
- Date and label the container
- Clean up and put away your equipment and tools.

CHAPTER 7: RECIPES

Follow directions as outlined in the 'how to' section, unless other directions are given.

SIMPLE LOTION

-2 oz. distilled water
-4 oz. oil
-2 oz. beeswax
-¼ teaspoon vitamin E oil
-Essential oil of your choice (dilute based on oil used)
-Germall Plus (0.1% to 0.5 % of the total formula) **OR** Otiphen Plus (0.75% to 1.5% of the total formula)

HAND AND BODY LOTION

- 8 oz. distilled water or aloe vera
- 4 oz. coconut oil
- 4 oz. shea butter
- 4 oz. beeswax
- Essential oil of your choice (dilute based on oil used)
- Germall Plus (0.1% to 0.5 % of the total formula) **OR** Otiphen Plus (0.75% to 1.5% of the total formula)

HONEY CINNAMON LOTION

-12 oz. distilled water or aloe vera gel
-1/2 teaspoon cinnamon
-6 oz. olive oil
-5 tablespoons beeswax
-1 teaspoon honey
-¼ teaspoon Vitamin E
-Germall Plus (0.1% to 0.5 % of the total formula) **OR** Otiphen Plus (0.75% to 1.5% of the total formula)

SIMPLE CREAM

-8 oz. distilled water or aloe vera
-4 oz. sweet almond oil
-4 oz. beeswax
-1 teaspoon vitamin e
-Essential oil of your choice (dilute based on oil used)
-Germall Plus (0.1% to 0.5 % of the total formula) **OR** Otiphen Plus (0.75% to 1.5% of the total formula)

HERBAL SELF-TANNING LOTION

-2 cups distilled water*
-6 tablespoons of green tea and dried linden leaf flowers*
-6 tablespoons sesame seed oil
-6 tablespoons avocado oil
-1 cup lanolin
-Essential oil of your choice (dilute based on oil used)
-Germall Plus (0.1% to 0.5 % of the total formula) **OR** Otiphen Plus (0.75% to 1.5% of the total formula)

*Make a strong tea with the green tea, linden and water. Let cool, then strain.

NATURAL SUNSCREEN & SUNBURN RESCUE

-6 oz. pure aloe vera gel
-12 oz. coconut oil
-6 oz. emulsifying wax
-3 capsules vitamin E oil, broken
-1 tablespoon zinc oxide ointment
-15 drops lavender essential oil
-5 drops wintergreen essential oil
-5 drops carrot seed essential oil
-Germall Plus (0.1% to 0.5 % of the total formula) **OR** Otiphen Plus (0.75% to 1.5% of the total formula)

LOTION BAR

-4 oz. part coconut oil
-4 oz. sweet almond oil
-4 oz. part beeswax
-1 teaspoon of vitamin E oil
-Essential oil of your choice (dilute based on oil used)
-Germall Plus (0.1% to 0.5 % of the total formula) **OR** Otiphen Plus (0.75% to 1.5% of the total formula)

ANTI-AGING LOTION BAR

-1 tablespoon avocado oil
-1 tablespoon coconut oil
-1 teaspoon mango butter
-2 teaspoons beeswax
-½ teaspoon vitamin e
-6 drops carrot seed oil
-4 drops comfrey oil
-8-10 drops lavender oil
-Germall Plus (0.1% to 0.5 % of the total formula) **OR** Otiphen Plus (0.75% to 1.5% of the total formula)

COCOA BUTTER LOTION BAR

-4 oz. cup beeswax
-4 oz. cocoa butter
-4 oz. coconut oil
-1 tablespoon almond oil
-1 Tablespoon jojoba oil
-Essential oil of your choice (dilute based on oil used)
-Germall Plus (0.1% to 0.5 % of the total formula) **OR** Otiphen Plus (0.75% to 1.5% of the total formula)

COCONUT BODY BUTTER

-4 oz. coconut oil
-2 oz. shea butter
-2 oz. olive oil
-2 oz. emulsifying wax
-Essential oil of your choice (dilute based on oil used)
-Germall Plus (0.1% to 0.5 % of the total formula) **OR** Otiphen Plus (0.75% to 1.5% of the total formula)

CHAPTER 8: HOW TO ADJUST BATCH SIZES

It becomes much easier to adjust recipes when you think of the recipe in terms of percentages. By thinking of the percentage of water, oil, and wax you need; it becomes easy to make a recipe of any size volume. Lotions are considered cosmetics and the measurements for ingredients are meant to be in weight not volume. You should always weigh ingredients on a digital scale if possible. Weighing ingredients ensures accuracy and accuracy ensures that you will be able to make a consistent lotion each and every time.

If you intend to sell or keep your lotion unrefrigerated for more than a week, you will need to add a preservative. There are many natural preservatives that you can add to your lotion that also have beneficial properties for skin protection, healing and hydration. Preservatives act as anti-oxidants for water and oil, preventing the growth of bacteria, mold and yeasts. Bacteria, mold and yeast can form in any mixture containing water, which is why it is so important to use clean safe distilled water, and to add a preservative.

Due to their antimicrobial and antiseptic properties, there are a couple of common preservatives you can use for oil and water emulsions:

-Germall Plus (0.1% to 0.5 % of the total formula)

-Otiphen Plus (0.75% to 1.5% of the total formula)

If you plan to sell your lotion and are unsure of how your clients will store your product, you can purchase stronger preservatives. Commercially available preservatives will ensure that your product will be shelf stable and resist growing yeasts, molds and bacteria. Your clients will still receive the benefits of your homemade lotions and creams without having to worry about any spoilage.

If you have any concerns about maintaining the consistency of your lotion when you increase or decrease your recipe, always re-do your math in the form of percentages.

CHAPTER 9: CREATING YOUR OWN RECIPES

By starting with some basic amounts, and beginning to think of your ingredients in terms of percentages, you can create your own recipes based on ingredients that you like. As you make more lotion and use them, you will begin to see and feel how they affect your skin. The following sample recipe is for a small, it is easily doubled or tripled depending on how much you want to make.

This is a recipe for a simple lotion. If you use oils that are liquid at room temperature you do not need to warm them, you can warm the lanolin just until it is liquid.

YOUR RECIPE WILL LOOK LIKE THIS:

-50% Oil
-25% Lanolin/Beeswax/Emulsifying Wax
-25% Water
-Trace: Vitamin E & Essential Oils

USING STANDARD MEASUREMENTS:

-4 oz. Oil
-2 oz. Lanolin/Beeswax/Emulsifying Wax
-2 oz. Water
-Trace: Vitamin E % Essential Oils
-Germall Plus (0.1% to 0.5 % of the total formula) **OR** Otiphen Plus (0.75% to 1.5% of the total formula)

When you break the recipe down, consider the properties and functions of each ingredient. Use ingredients that you like and are familiar with.

-4 oz. Oil

You can use any oil that you like: olive, sesame, almond, apricot kernel oil, coconut or grape seed, are some suggestions. Use organic oils when possible, as your skin does absorb the compounds in the oil. Organic oils are best for your skin, as they do not contain harmful pesticides.

-2 oz. Lanolin/Beeswax/Emulsifying Wax

Lanolin has amazing moisturizing and skin protective qualities. Lanolin forms a barrier that prevents moisture from escaping from the skin. Lanolin will give your lotion a smooth creamy consistency. Beeswax has a warm color, a sweet aroma and lends a very silky feel to your lotions. Emulsifying wax is usually odorless and very mild; it works to combine the oils and water without lending any characteristics like lanolin or beeswax.

-2 oz. Water

Always use distilled water. If you cannot use distilled water, boil your water for 10 minutes. Boiling your water will kill any bacteria that could have a harmful effect on your lotion.

-Vitamin E

Use Vitamin E as an antioxidant and as a preservative to extend the shelf life of your lotion. Use at a rate of 0.04% for the oils in your lotion. In this recipe with 75% or 6 oz. of oil you will need to use 0.25 of an ounce.

-Essential Oils

You can use any Essential Oil or any combination of essential oils that you like. You can choose essential oils for their aromas or their skin nourishing properties. Depending on the essential oils you choose you will need to look up their concentration and determine how much essential oil to use.

-Germall Plus (0.1% to 0.5 % of the total formula) **OR** Otiphen Plus (0.75% to 1.5% of the total formula)

CHAPTER 10: FAQ'S

IS THERE A STANDARD RECIPE FOR HOMEMADE LOTION?

There is no standard recipe for homemade lotion. Different lotion recipes will give you different types of lotion. If you change the amount of water or the types of oils, it will change the consistency and feel of your lotion.

WHAT'S THE BEST WAY TO MAKE LOTIONS AT HOME?

Lotion is very simple to make. In just a few minutes you can make a soothing, regenerating lotion to heal and repair your skin. Once you've made a batch of lotion you will realize how inferior commercially made lotions are. You will begin making lotion or creams by: Cleaning and sanitizing your workspace, Cleaning and sanitizing your equipment, tools and containers, Gathering all of your ingredients, Measuring all of your ingredients, Melting your oils, Melting your emulsifying agent or wax, Warming your water, Combine all of your ingredients in one mixing container, Using the immersion blender, blend the lotion (very gently so you don't introduce air into the mixture), Pour the lotion into containers, Allow the lotion to cool, then date and label, Clean up and put away your equipment and tools.

MY LOTION IS GREASY. CAN I FIX IT?

You can add some cornstarch to absorb some of the oils and reduce the greasy after touch. Make a note on your recipe and reduce the amount of oil you use the next time you make that particular lotion recipe.

DO I HAVE TO BUY AN EMULSIFYING WAX TO MAKE LOTION?

No. You do not. You can use beeswax and lanolin to bind your oil and water mixtures together.

DO I HAVE TO BUY COMMERCIAL PRESERVATIVES TO MAKE LOTION?

By following strict sanitation protocols and adding vitamin and tea tree oil, you can safely prevent bacteria from growing in your lotions. Make small batches of lotions and use small jars to store it in. By storing your product in a cool place you will reduce the risks of your lotions going bad. If your lotions do grow mold, or turn rancid, discard them immediately.

Printed in Great Britain
by Amazon